Farther Than 26.2 Miles

Running brought us together...
Running separated us...
And Running is how I survived it all...

Cheryl Collins Gatons

Palmetto Publishing Group
Charleston, SC

First Edition

Printed in the United States

ISBN-13: 978-1-64111-468-4
ISBN-10: 1-64111-468-1

Dedication

To my two biggest fans and the most important men in my life:

My husband, Kevin, who will always be the "love of my life" and who lives on through our three amazing children: Sydney, Quintin, and Lillian.

And

My dad, John, who taught me to never doubt myself. . . . I was so blessed to have you as my dad.

I remember saying to my mom shortly after Kevin died, "I wish he never ran." And my mom replied, "But you never would have met him."

This is my story of how I grew up believing you could actually plan your life and it would work out according to that plan if you were a good person and made good choices, or so I thought.

Table of Contents

Foreword ·ix
1   Glass Half Full · 1
2   Life Would Never Be the Same · 4
3   The Ride Home · 7
4   The Darkest Days of My Life · 9
5   Final Goodbye · 14
6   Running for the Fun of It · 17
7   Running with a Purpose · 21
8   Meeting Kevin · 25
9   Our First Date · 28
10 1996 Olympic Marathon Trials · · · · · · · · · · · · · · · · · · · 31
11 My Personal Life Was Taking Off Too · · · · · · · · · · · · · 37
12 World Games · 41
13 The Next Step · 45
14 New Partner in Life and in Training · · · · · · · · · · · · · · · 54
15 Sydney, Australia · 60
16 Life Was Good · 65
17 November 3, 2006 · 70
18 ARVD (a.k.a. ARVC) · 73
19 My New Reality · 77
20 The Children · 86
21 More Heartache · 95
22 How I Survived It All · 101
23 The Other Side · 113
24 Running Until I Cross the Finish Line · · · · · · · · · · · · · · 118
Acknowledgments · 124
A Special Acknowledgement: · 131

Foreword

This is a story of a very special wife, mother, and athlete. I have had the opportunity to coach running for fifty years at all levels, high school, college, and post-collegiate. During my career, I have had the privilege to coach the top American female finisher in the 1984, 1992, and 2008 Olympic marathon. I have also had the opportunity to watch the evolution of women's running to a place where today we have more women than men running road races throughout the US. The last couple of years, women have had much more success at the international level than our male athletes.

Cheryl never took running seriously in high school, and her husband once told her that she would have been the worst athlete to coach while she was in high school. This was probably true, but once she fell in love with running, she became the most coachable athlete I have ever dealt with during my career.

I once made the statement that I would never coach an athlete over the phone, as I have always believed it is very important to be in the space of your athletes. Cheryl gave me a call in 1997, and we agreed to meet at the Tufts 10K and discuss her coaching situation with help from Joe Sarver, her running advisor in Pittsburgh. Watching her run the 10K, realizing how special her running mechanics were, and after meeting Cheryl and realizing how special she was as an individual, I could not refuse to help her with her running.

Both Joe Sarver and I still advise Cheryl, and I still give her workouts on Sundays whenever she is training for a race. I take very little credit with Cheryl's athletic success, as she never fails to complete a weekly plan, and she is always eager for what is coming the following week. In all the years I have helped her with her running, she has never failed to complete a workout. When training for an upcoming goal, she is as focused at age fifty as she was at age twenty-eight. Being a very special mother, she has the unique ability to balance her responsibilities as a single parent and her running.

Cheryl's story is one of tremendous sadness, mental strength, and athletic success. The most important part of her journey has been that of a single parent and mother. Her children are very special and represent her excellence as a role model and mother. Cheryl Collins Gatons is one of those very special individuals who cross your path in life and help make you a much better person.

Bob Sevene
Coach

1
Glass Half Full

I was born on November 8, 1966, along with my twin sister, Suzanne. My family was a typical Beaver Cleaver family. My mom, Susanne, stayed home and took care of the five of us (my older sister, Laura; my twin sister, Suzanne; me, my younger brother, Jeff; and my younger sister, Jennifer), while my dad, John, started his own company, the John J. Collins Company. We were a typical middle-class family that lived in Plum Boro, Pennsylvania (a suburb outside of Pittsburgh). Our home was a basic two-story with one full bath. My twin sister and I shared a room as did my older and younger sisters while my brother had his own. It was a simple house full of the chaos of five children and love.

We all loved one another, and my parents truly loved each other until the day my dad died in 2007. Of course, we fought on occasion like all siblings do, but we were all good kids. None of us had drug or alcohol problems, and we grew up with high Catholic values.

Our dad would kiss our mom goodbye every morning and hello every evening. Our mom would make sure we ate all of our fruits and vegetables and drank lots of milk. Even when we were running late for school, we had to drink our orange juice and eat a good breakfast. Our dad would tell us stories about "Herman the Mouse," (a character he made up who lived in our woods and protected us,) and he would play Speed Racer. All five of us would get in our 1965 green Mustang convertible, and he would pretend he was Speed Racer. Every night, we would anxiously wait for him to get home and run down and hug and kiss him. We loved playing with our dad and hearing his Herman the Mouse stories. Herman became our best friend.

Our mom not only made sure we ate right, but she also made sure we were always dressed well. She would blast music, especially Elvis, in the kitchen all day long, and she took us to a lot of concerts as children.

We played kickball, hopscotch, two-square, run down, hide-and-seek, jump rope, and rode our bikes until the streetlights came on. Every evening, we ate dinner as a family. We all participated in afterschool activities, but weekends were about family, church, catechism, and Saturday-morning cartoons.

Life was simple and good. We never heard of dysfunction, and we were blessed. We all did well in school and were never asked if we were going to college. It was just assumed. We all did go on to college, get good jobs, and marry wonderful people. Just like life was meant to work out. We all grew up looking at the glass half full and looking at life through rose-colored glasses. Was this a good thing? Or did it make me unable to handle life's disappointments as well as those who didn't grow up this way? I'm not sure, but one thing I am sure of is that the glass isn't only half full; it can also be half empty.

Collins family. Bottom row (L–R): younger sister, Jennifer; mom, Susanne; dad, John. Top row (L–R): twin sister, Suzanne; me; brother, Jeff; older sister, Laura.

2

Life Would Never Be the Same

On November 3, 2006, in a single heartbeat, life as I knew it to be was no longer. It was completely taken away with a single phone call. Kevin, my husband of eight years, collapsed and died. Our dream of growing old together, raising our three children (Sydney, Quintin, and Lillian) together, having more children, and so many of our other dreams died along with him.

Kevin died while navigating the Hershey State Cross Country course. He was showing Samantha, a runner he coached who had qualified for the state meet, the course the day before the big race.

I remember thinking, *Wait, this can't be for real. No, stop! This wasn't part of our plan. We were supposed to grow old together, raise our three children together. 'Til death do us part. This wasn't supposed to happen now, but forty years from now. This wasn't what I was brought up believing. Life would work out if you made good choices, and I did by marrying Kevin on August 8, 1998. He wasn't just a good choice; he was the perfect choice for me.*

Why did the person I fall in love with have to die young? So many questions. Why take a young, loving husband and father? Why did our children have to grow up without their dad? Why did I have to become a widow at such a young age and never get to share our children's special moments with their dad? Why? Never in a million years did I think I would be or want to be a single parent. *Never* would I have chosen this path.

I guess one thing I did learn was that I can't plan my life. It is God's plan, and someday I will understand this plan once I see Kevin again. I might not like this plan, but for some reason, it is the path my life took. So, in the meantime, I need to make the most of it. I too realized that things just happen. Good and bad, that is life. You have to take the good with the bad. It isn't God punishing you. It has nothing to do with you as a person. It's just life.

The day started out like any other day. Kevin got ready to go teach and gave me a hug and kiss as he did each day. I then got Sydney, our oldest, ready for half-day kindergarten. She had just turned six on Halloween. Our Halloween baby who we loved. Once she went to school, I ran with the other two—Quintin, who was three, and Lillian, who was twenty-one months—in the baby jogger.

Afterward, I spoke with Kevin as he headed to the high school to get in the van to head to the course. He said he loved me. I said the same. I asked him to call later tonight, and there was an odd hesitation, followed by the words, "Okay, if I can." He had never said that before. Now, looking back, I fixate on that and wonder if deep down inside he knew what was to come.

I got Sydney off the bus, and the four of us headed to Pittsburgh to a play area and plans for dinner later. As we were getting out of the car and I was setting up the double stroller for Quintin and Lillian, my cell phone rang.

Sydney said, "Mommy, your phone," but, of course, I couldn't find it in time.

When I saw a missed call from Hutchinson Elementary, the school where Kevin taught, I immediately became concerned. Why would they call me? Kevin was on his way to Hershey. They would only call if he had been in an accident.

I called back and asked to speak to the principal. He answered, and I quickly asked, "What happened to Kevin? Was he in an accident?" I rambled off questions in a panicked voice.

Mr. Mansfield kept asking me where the children and I were, never answering my questions about Kevin.

Finally, I screamed, "Oh my God! He died, didn't he?"

Mr. Mansfield again asked where we were.

I am not even sure if he came out and told me Kevin had died. I went on to find out later from Mr. Mansfield that he struggled with delivering the news not only because he cared about Kevin as a colleague and friend, but because he also felt tremendous responsibility, being the one to deliver the life-altering news.

I simply said, "I am heading home." Crying hysterically, I got the children back in the car. Sydney understood my distress. Two women whom I didn't know—other than that they were kind Samaritans—asked if I needed help. I said sadly that my husband had just died. They looked shocked and simply helped all of us into the car.

Sydney knew something was wrong. Why was Mommy crying? What had happened? Lillian and Quintin recognized my sadness, but they had no idea how quickly all of our lives had just changed. If only I had never called back, life would be okay. The kids and I would go to the play area, never knowing, as we were driving to have fun, that their daddy had died. It was approximately three o'clock in the afternoon, and suddenly our lives were forever altered. The day started out normal, but by 3:00 p.m., everything as I knew it to be changed forever.

My first instinct was to head home. The children and I would then be okay. I couldn't wait for someone to come and get us as so many had wanted us to do. They feared I might wreck over being so distraught. However, my first reaction was to escape this place where I got the horrible, life-altering news and head home.

3

The Ride Home

Once in the car, I made sure the children were okay and saw how confused they were, especially Sydney. What had just happened? This had to be a bad dream. No way could Kevin have died. It didn't make sense. He'd been perfectly healthy-looking that morning. How could things change so quickly? As I had these confusing thoughts, I immediately called my best friend and twin sister, Suzanne. She is the one I always turn to in moments of need, and I now needed her more than ever. She lives in California, and when she answered, I said, "He's gone."

She could tell by my voice something horrible had happened, but she asked me, "Who?"

I said, "Kevin."

She screamed and cried while saying that she and her family would be on a plane and with the children and me tomorrow. I knew I could depend on her to help the children and me through this most difficult time. I then called Kevin's parents and asked if it was true. His mom said yes. I begged them to please be at our house when I got there. I felt they would understand my pain and we could grieve together. Next were my mom and dad, who, by the sound of their voices, already knew. Kevin's parents had called them, looking for me, after Mr. Mansfield had called them when he couldn't get a hold of me. My parents told me they would be at our house.

To this day, I am not sure how I got home. I just drove and kept telling Sydney that we would be okay. I'm not sure if she believed it because I didn't believe it myself. As I got closer, more and more people called, offering to come and get me.

Coach Snider, who had been with Kevin, called and wanted me to speak to the doctor who had worked on Kevin.

The doctor said, "I am so sorry. We tried everything to save him."

It was like a line out of a horrible nightmare. I thanked him to comfort him because he sounded devastated too, knowing that a young husband and father had just left a wife and three young children behind.

Coach Snider wanted me to speak with the doctor in hopes of finding peace. He and Kevin shared a special friendship. Kevin contributed the coach he became too him. Kevin admired him not only as a coach but for the person he was. Coach Snider later told me it was the worst day of his life as well.

I still didn't completely know all the details. He collapsed, got immediate help, and died. I would find out more later.

As the children and I approached the house, several people ran toward the car to get us out. They were just thankful we were home safe. Along with about twenty people on our lawn, I remember looking for his mom and dad and feeling a sense of relief that they were there to grieve with me. As the children were helped out of the car, Dave Zilli, the high school principal, helped me. I think I finally collapsed and could no longer be strong for our children. He carried me into the house as his parents—at least, I think they were his parents—went with the children.

It truly was the worst day of my life. How could a day start off so wonderfully and end so terribly?

4

The Darkest Days of My Life

Once inside, reality set in. Kevin was no longer coming home. This was no longer our home where we were to raise our children and grow old together.

I remember being taken to a couch and so many people being there. I just sat, kind of taking it all in while being half out of it. I remember people saying that they were so sorry about Kevin and people bringing in food and drinks. It was almost bizarre in this devastating moment that so many people were in our house. The children were taken upstairs and being taken care of while still kind of being oblivious to the full impact of that phone call. His parents were solemn and devastated too. Kevin's mom wanted to start making plans, I think to keep busy and not allow her mind to really go to that dark, sad place. She asked which funeral home I wanted to use.

Which funeral home? I thought to myself (maybe out loud). That was never even spoken about between Kevin and me. We probably— no, I know—we assumed that someday we would talk about it, but not now. We were too young. It really never crossed our minds.

I chose Pantalone's because the stepdad of Jeff Hite, a former runner that Kevin coached, owned it. Kevin always spoke so highly about Jeff, so I felt it was a good choice. A choice Kevin would be okay with.

I just remember really wanting my parents to get there. I wanted them to hug me and make me feel like things would be okay, just like they did when I was a little girl. I needed my mom and dad so badly in that moment. I was so relieved once they came and once Rick, Kevin's and my good friend, got there to comfort me. Their presence made me feel safer. I was so frightened in those moments and so afraid of life now without Kevin. Rick agreed to pick out the suit Kevin would wear, and his mom wanted him to be buried in his favorite slippers. Kevin could be such an old soul at times, and he loved his slippers. I could just picture him in them, which made me cry. Everything made me cry. . . .

As for the eulogies, I asked Rick to do one and Coach Snider, whom Kevin coached with, to do another. They both knew Kevin extremely well and at different periods of his life. My older sister, Laura, came, and so did my brother, Jeff. At one point, Laura asked everyone to please leave except for family. It was overwhelming to me and Kevin's family to have so many people, including strangers, with us in this tragic moment. We needed to grieve alone. It was just too much.

Kathy and Paul, my very good friends from college, arrived. I hugged them and cried. They were safe to show how I felt to. Paul later went on to tell me that I had pounded on his chest so hard while crying and saying, "I can't believe he died." Looking back, I showed more emotion to those I was comfortable with.

Another good friend from college, Tom, came to comfort me too. I eventually wanted to be alone in our room and grieve. Laura and Kathy stayed the night because I was so afraid to be alone. I'm not exactly sure of what I was afraid of though. I was petrified, maybe, of what was to come: my new life without Kevin.

The next day was horrific—waking up, knowing this was for real. I wasn't having a bad dream. This was my new reality. Kevin was gone. I had to go and pick out a casket at the funeral home and start making funeral plans. This was just the beginning of the horrible things I would have to do now with Kevin being gone. I look back now, and I don't even know how I survived those first days. Thank goodness for my family and close friends. His mom and dad had a spare plot in my mother-in-law's family cemetery. A plot was another thing Kevin and I had never discussed or thought about along with making funeral arrangements. We had, at least we thought, another forty years to do that.

Kevin died on Friday, November 3, 2006, in Hershey, Pennsylvania. His body wasn't brought to the funeral home until Monday. They had to perform an autopsy since he died at the young age of forty-six. It was Dauphin County's requirement. Jeff, his former athlete, went to get the body. He said he talked to Kevin the whole ride back. I found comfort in that. I worried those first few days when he was in Hershey all alone. I didn't want Kevin to be alone. I wanted to be there with him to hug him. I didn't want him to be afraid. I know it sounds crazy. He was deceased, but I was still acting like a concerned and loving wife.

That weekend was the longest and weirdest weekend of my life. I tried to keep life as normal as possible for our children while in the back of my mind (more like the forefront) anxiously waiting for Kevin's body to return home. How could I pretend life was normal? It was anything but normal. Fortunately, my twin sister, Suzanne, and her children made the weekend easier to get through. Children do live in the moment. Sydney, Quintin, and Lillian had fun with their cousins.

Monday, November 6, finally got here. It was the night that our families would get to see Kevin and say our goodbyes. It was terrifying. I didn't want to enter the room and see Kevin that way. Seeing him that way would make it all real. All so final. He really did die. Plus, I was afraid to see Kevin lying there in the casket. Monsignor, who had been a tremendous support since the day Kevin died, agreed to enter the room with me. I didn't want to do it alone. I was scared, not sure of what I would see. Monsignor was a calming presence. He made me feel safe, maybe because he was the closest person to God. Kevin didn't look like himself. He didn't look like the Kevin I had seen leave on Friday morning. Monsignor made me feel better by saying, "He doesn't look like the Kevin you know because he is no longer here. His soul has moved on." That made how Kevin looked easier to accept.

Tuesday, November 7, was to be an all-day viewing from 2:00 p.m. until 10:00 p.m. I only wanted one day of viewing because I knew it would be painful for all of us. It was the longest and most depressing and sad day. So many people came to pay their respects to Kevin. Kevin was well known in the small town of Greensburg. He'd grown up here, had gone to college close by, and then had coached and taught here. Over one thousand people came to say goodbye: family, friends, former and current coworkers, former and current athletes he'd coached, cross-country teams and coaches from all over. One of his very good running friends, Dave, said he stood in line to pay his respects longer than it took him to run a marathon. Another close running friend of Kevin's said that they came to pay their respects to Kevin but also came because they were deeply concerned about the children and me.

My coach, Joe Sarver, kept checking on me and giving me milkshakes to stay nourished. There were moments where I stood for long periods and moments where I just needed to sit. I only left the line once to go to the restroom. Nat Pantalone, the owner of the funeral home, kept checking on me also and made me take a break.

My dad, whose back had been hurting him, brought a mutual friend of ours, Harry, over to me. When I saw Harry, I began to cry. Harry was how Kevin and I had met. Harry simply said, "I am so sorry." He said this as if he were taking the blame for the path my life was going down now.

I told him it wasn't his fault. I made a good choice in marrying Kevin. He was my soul mate. I thought again to myself, *Why did the person I choose to fall in love with have to die young?* He was only forty-six. Kevin walked out the door and never came home. How could this be? We were both competitive runners. He took care of himself. He was the epitome of health. If you lined him up next to ten other men his age, you would never guess he would die young. From the phone call to this very long day life was a living hell. Pantalone's was wonderful in helping to make this process as bearable as possible. The pain was so debilitating. I was completely devastated, and my heart was broken. I actually recall someone saying to me, "I now know what a broken heart looks like." That's how sad and empty I looked.

I was only able to get through the first few days with the love of family and close friends. Not only was I lost, I was also scared about how this had become my life, our life, and our children's lives.

5
Final Goodbye

O*ne more horrible day,* I told myself. If I could just get through the funeral, somehow life might get back to normal. What exactly would be normal now? Would life ever be normal again?

After the children and I said our final goodbyes, I kissed and hugged Kevin one last time. How I wanted for him to hug and kiss me back, making this all go away. I then placed our wedding photo in his casket along with a card telling him I would never stop loving him and I would never, despite "'til death do us part," really part from him. For he would forever be the love of my life and own part of my heart. I was given his wedding ring and then sadly waited outside the room while others said their goodbyes.

As I sat on the bench outside the room, I looked outside through the glass front door and saw a woman running. I thought to myself, *How can she be running*? My world had stopped, and she was going on with her life. Not deliberately, I realized. It was just life. Mine would never be the same, and she had no idea of that as she ran. At that moment, I wanted to be that woman running, running away from this new reality, this new life without Kevin.

After one last goodbye, I wasn't prepared to never see Kevin again. The children and I got in the limo behind the hearse. We headed to the church for the funeral mass. Again, I found myself going through the motions for the sake of the children. They still didn't quite understand the full ramifications of that day.

As we pulled up to the cathedral, I noticed an honor guard formed by his fellow teachers and some friends. His colleagues were all able to attend. Mr. Mansfield, the principal who had told me the news, had made sure all could attend. The honor guard was a beautiful gesture. I started to cry. I carried Lilly, who was twenty-one months at the time. As I entered the church behind the casket, dressed in all black, I was overcome with emotion and disbelief again that this was really my life. My already limp body became even weaker. The children eventually went downstairs to play with their cousins while we said goodbye to their daddy upstairs.

My good friend Sally later told me that she knew I would be okay because she said I looked as pretty as I did on our wedding day. I wanted to look pretty as his bride, starting our lives together, and I now wanted to look pretty for him as his widow, ending our lives together here on earth.

The service was long and beautiful, but all I can remember is holding tightly to the fabric that draped the casket, not wanting to let go of the cloth, of Kevin, or of our life together.

The eulogies were both touching and, in some ways, funny. Rick, his lifelong friend, gave a beautiful eulogy about Kevin's childhood. Then there was Coach Snider's eulogy. It, too, was beautiful, but spot on describing the adult Kevin. At one point, he said he would never forget how at one race, when the gun went off, Kevin was in the Porta-John. The next thing he remembered was seeing Kevin go running by and on to win the race. Everyone who knew Kevin knew he was a gentleman while also being an extremely intense competitor. During that part, for a brief moment, everyone laughed. Then a silent sadness overcame the cathedral again. I am so grateful for the two of them for honoring Kevin the way they did.

After the service, as I waited in the limo for the final procession to the cemetery, I will never forget Mrs. Briggs, the mother of my lifelong friend Bobby, saying to me, "No one your age should ever have to go through this." Honestly, I wish this on no one at any age. It was horrific.

The funeral ended up being on November 8, which ironically was my fortieth birthday. It was all bad. I remember being the last one in the cemetery with Nat Pantalone, the funeral director. I didn't want to say goodbye, goodbye forever. I cried as the casket was lowered into the ground. I kissed it one last time and placed a rose on it. My heart wasn't broken; it was shattered. I had just buried the love of my life, the father of my children, and my future.

I saw a friend of mine walking off holding hands with her husband. How I would have given anything for that to be Kevin and me.

6
Running for the Fun of It

Back to my days at Plum High School, where my twin sister, Suzanne, and I joined the track team for the social aspect. The coach told me I would be running the mile and Suzanne the two-mile (she cried, as I was relieved). I did okay running the mile. I eventually ran a five-minute-thirty-second mile while not caring at all.

A large number of us would hide at the local bowling alley when we were supposed to be running, or we would sneak off and watch *Guiding Light*. I never ran except during track season (that is if I ran at all), and I never cared. It was just about having fun.

One year, I made it to the Western Pennsylvania Interscholastic Athletic League (WPIAL) finals. My coach came to get me to run a few days before with another athlete. I ran to the bottom of my street and dead seriously told him, "I needed to go home and get ready for our school's Kennywood Picnic (a well-known amusement park in Pittsburgh)." I did just that—turned around and ran home. The coach was mad, but I cared more about Kennywood then WPIAL finals.

Many years later, Kevin said after hearing this, "You would have been the worst athlete to coach." At that point in my life, yes. I wasn't serious, just running for fun. I had no idea what was to come later with my running.

In college, I found myself running after a long day of electrical engineering labs and classes. It was my stress reliever. I would often run on the cross-country course, and this is where my love of running really began.

In 1985, there were only a few women in the field of electrical engineering. I had attended undecided orientation because I hadn't figured out what I wanted to major in. I had always loved and excelled in math, and with my dad's forward thinking and encouragement, I thought I would try electrical engineering. He felt it was the perfect career choice for a young, ambitious woman. He also felt it would be easier to start in electrical engineering then to transfer in later; I could always switch to a different major if I didn't like it. When we both met with the head of the engineering department, he accepted me into the program.

I loved engineering in college. It was fun to be of the minority, and I loved the challenges it offered. I was happy with my choice and had aspirations of eventually climbing the corporate ladder.

After college, my love for running continued to grow, especially when I moved to Newport Beach, California, for a job opportunity with Westinghouse. The weather was so perfect all the time; I wanted to spend every free moment outside. If only my experience as a young female engineer with Westinghouse was as perfect. It wasn't all bad, but most of the older male engineers weren't as forward-thinking as my dad. I found myself being discouraged at times. Often, I would give a suggestion or my opinion about a project and it would go unnoticed.

Suzanne joined Westinghouse a few months later, but with a different department, and her experience was a little different. Her group, unlike mine, consisted mostly of young male engineers who were open-minded to a female counterpart.

I did have a great manager, Barry, who tried to groom me, and Mark, another young engineer, who supported my efforts. However, in 1990, I found it overall to be very much an old boys' club.

Eventually, I quit my job and took on a variety of other jobs, but I sometimes wonder if I had started with a different company, would my love of electrical engineering have continued? Suzanne did stick it out with Westinghouse.

We both loved living in California and loved being outside, whether it was at the beach rollerblading, biking, or running a route to and around Balboa Island. We couldn't get enough of the great weather.

Eventually, we started running the Back Bay, a ten-mile loop, each evening after work. I wanted to run with her and talk, but she didn't want to talk, so I started running ahead with my Walkman. When she would be off with Jay, her boyfriend at the time and now her husband, I would go for a second run, oftentimes to Corona Del Mar and back. On that route, I would run down to the beach, across the beach, back up the hill, and home. Another route I would often do was part of the Back Bay; I would end up on a high school track, where I would run a mile or so all out, then head home. On Sunday nights, I would run to Balboa Island, around the island, and home fast, never realizing that I was kind of doing a speed workout. I just loved to run and loved running all out at times.

I remember times when I ran the Back Bay, I would see a woman about my age running who looked like a really good runner, and I subconsciously wished I was her, never really thinking that someday that might be me.

I lived in California for four years, and my love of running grew and grew. I was running simply for the fun of it.

In 1994, I decided to move home. I missed my mom and dad and wanted to be closer to them and the rest of my family. Once home, my love of running continued.

There have been times after Kevin died that I thought if I had never moved home, I would have been spared of so much heartache and pain, but on the other side, I would have missed out on so much *joy*.

7

Running with a Purpose

Once home, my dad and other family members didn't quite understand why I loved to run so much. What was the purpose?

My brother, Jeff, decided to challenge me to a race. It was a 5K in the evening at North Park. He, too, kind of thought all my running was silly.

Not being a competitive runner, I had no idea to taper before a race. I actually went out that morning and ran my normal eight miles. That evening, I headed to North Park to meet my brother and sister-in-law, Carla, at the race. My brother lined up beside me, and when the gun went off, he sprinted out as if he were going to win the whole race. I laughed and let him go because he really thought he could beat me. I ran with my Walkman, and at the turnaround, I was winning the female race. I couldn't believe it. I saw Carla, and she looked good. My brother started to look tired. I cheered him on and kept running. I ended up winning the female race in eighteen minutes and eighteen seconds. Carla came in not too long after and then, finally, my brother. We teased him that a woman with a baby jogger beat him. I really didn't think I would win. After that race, my brother, along with my mom and dad, understood why I ran so much.

People asked me at the awards ceremony what college I ran for. I told them I didn't run for a college. I was twenty-eight years old and simply running for the fun of it. They also asked me what racing flats I wore. What are racing flats? I just ran to run.

A couple of weeks later, my brother-in-law, Joe, took me to a 5K in Butler, Pennsylvania. At that race, he told me I couldn't wear my Walkman. "Real runners don't run races with one."

I told him I didn't think I could run without my music, but I decided to try. The gun went off, and despite my slipping at the turn-around (it was raining), I went on to win overall for the women again in eighteen minutes and eighteen seconds. Now my whole family looked at my running differently. I even began thinking that maybe I was good at running. So, I decided to get some answers to all those questions and help in regards to my running.

I called Mike Radley, who was the race director for the Great Race. The Great Race is a big 10K race in Pittsburgh, Pennsylvania. He told me to call Joe Sarver, who held running clinics. (If Mike had never suggested my calling Joe, who knows where I would have gone with my running. Thank you, Mike.) I called Joe, and he told me he was extremely busy with work, grad school, and a young family. So, he couldn't help me at this time. No sooner had I hung up than the phone rang again. It was Joe, calling back to tell me to meet him at the Carnegie Mellon University (CMU) track. He was concerned that I might get ruined by someone's bad coaching.

A couple of days later, I met him at the CMU track. Joe looked like a long-distance runner. He greeted me with a warm, friendly smile and had this positive energy about him. Immediately, I felt comfortable with him and knew I could trust him with my running. He had me run some quarter-repeats (four hundred meters) to see what kind of leg speed I had. After I ran the repeats, Joe said to me, "I can get you qualified for the Olympic trials in the marathon in just six weeks' time."

He wanted me to run the Columbus Marathon, which was six weeks away. I initially thought he was a little crazy, but he seemed to believe in me. Joe felt that I had a high enough mileage base and just needed to do a couple long runs (twenty-milers) and speed workouts to fine-tune my running before the Columbus Marathon. So, over the next six weeks, we met and did some twenty-mile runs along with some speed workouts. This was all new to me. Joe made it all so easy. During the twenty-mile runs, our coach/athlete relationship really started to grow. It was so natural, the connection between us.

Joe helped me through the speed workouts by making them fun. He was faster than me, so we would play cat and mouse. He would give me a lead, and I would have to try to hold him off. I instantly looked up to him and respected him as a coach while knowing that with his guidance, my running would take off.

Race day came fast. I lined up with the six-minute-thirty-second-mile pace group, since in 1994 the qualifying time was two hours and fifty minutes or faster. I ran the first mile in seven minutes to be conservative.

I ran with Steve, another runner who wanted to run two hours and fifty minutes. He was kind enough to agree to pace me. At mile fifteen, I remember saying to him that I felt good and was going to take off. He said to go.

At mile twenty-one, Joe gave me the thumbs-up and said I was on pace to qualify. I smiled and kept running. I did go on to qualify in two hours, forty-six minutes, and thirty-three seconds and placed seventh overall. I hugged Joe and called my family in disbelief.

My dad was especially thrilled for me. I could hear the excitement and pride in his voice. Suddenly, I went from the girl running for fun to the girl who had just qualified for the Olympic trials in the marathon. How quickly everything had changed, just like on November 3, 2006. Sometimes, I wonder if I had never moved home and if my brother had never challenged me to that race, would I still be the girl just running for the fun of it?

8
Meeting Kevin

After the 1994 Columbus Marathon, I was thrown into the world of competitive running, where, eventually, I would meet Kevin. I ran some local races, which I won. Then I thought I would try the Pittsburgh Marathon. The first time I ran it, I placed tenth overall and ran two hours, forty-two minutes, and forty-three seconds. I would continue to run local races and win, never knowing a handsome runner had his eye on me.

In the fall of 1995, I returned to the Columbus Marathon. Joe Sarver was running the whole marathon, and I was running fifteen miles of it as a training run with him to get ready for the 1996 Olympic marathon trials, which would be held that February in Columbia, South Carolina. Little did I know I would meet the handsome runner who had been seeing me at local races. That handsome runner was Kevin Gatons. He, too, was a competitive runner and had gone to Columbus in the hopes of qualifying for the marathon Olympic trials. He had run two hours and twenty-four minutes that previous summer at Grandma's Marathon and missed qualifying by a couple minutes. The men's standard was two hours and twenty-two minutes or faster.

I didn't know who Kevin was. Harry, our mutual friend, would often talk about him, and my dear running friend Christina Skarvelis liked him. I guess he had seen me at some local races and told Harry that the wrong runner liked him. I ended up meeting Kevin briefly before the race. Harry introduced us. Kevin had a green turtleneck on with a white sweatshirt turned inside-out. When Harry said that was Kevin and pointed him out to me, I immediately thought that if that guy liked me, oh my goodness. He was so handsome with piercing blue eyes. He looked like a young Robert Redford.

After we were introduced, we made small talk. I remember being nervous around him. I made some dumb comment, "Oh we both have the same racing flats [Nike Air Streaks] on." I wished him good luck, and we went our separate ways. It was a terribly cold day, and the wind chills were in the negatives. Not a very good day for anyone to qualify.

I remember being glad to reach fifteen miles and able to head back to the hotel while Joe went on to finish the marathon. As I was getting back to the hotel, I ran into Kevin. He had dropped, along with so many others, due to the weather conditions. The weather conditions wouldn't allow him to get a qualifying time, so he wanted to save it for another day.

I went up to shower, and later on, Chris and I returned to the hotel lobby. Chris saw Kevin and his friends and wanted to talk to him. As we were talking to him, another runner who I liked at the time came over, lifted me up, and gave me a big hug. In that moment, all I could think was, *Please, not in front of Kevin*, which, looking back, was odd. I had just met Kevin.

As we headed back to Pittsburgh, I told Chris if she didn't pursue Kevin, I would. I later told Harry, our mutual friend, what I had told Chris. Harry went on to tell Kevin. Kevin got my phone number from another runner. He kept the sticky note with my number on it in his wallet 'til he died. I still have it.

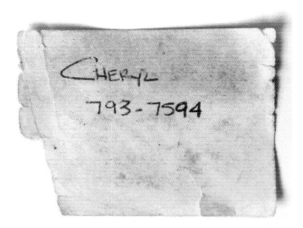

Kevin told Harry he was going to call me, and Harry passed along the news. A week or so later, Harry said Kevin wasn't going to call since Chris and I were friends and he didn't want to cause any trouble with our friendship.

When Harry told me this, my heart felt like it literally dropped. I thought to myself, *Why am I so sad? I don't even really know Kevin.* As November went on, Kevin found out that Chris was okay with him calling me, and I made sure she was okay with it too. So, he finally called.

9

Our First Date

Kevin called and asked me to meet him at the Balcony in Shadyside for dinner. As I sat there, waiting for Kevin, I befriended an older gentleman named Charles. We talked, and I told him I was meeting Kevin for our first date. He was an extremely nice and interesting man.

Suddenly, Kevin entered the restaurant a little frazzled since he was a few minutes late. He looked so handsome in a blue button-down dress shirt—it made his eyes stand out even more—and a pair of khakis.

I introduced him to Charles. Charles kept referring to him as my fiancé, and I told him no, it was our first date. We then said our goodbyes as he went to his table and us to ours. We laughed about how Charles called Kevin my fiancé.

We were eating upstairs, overlooking Walnut Street. I will never forget Charles looking up at us from outside, waving to us, and almost disappearing into the night. Was he meant to be there to bring Kevin and me together?

The night ended with Kevin walking me to my car, and I thanked him and gave him a kiss on the cheek. That began our relationship.

Kevin invited me to some Christmas parties that his friends were having following our first date. I can vividly see us driving through the Regent Square area and snow coming down as Mariah Carey's song "All I Want for Christmas Is You" blasted on the radio.

At that moment, I knew he was the one. It was easy to fall in love with Kevin. He had all the qualities I wanted in a husband. Our love of running brought us together, but it wasn't just the cute runner I fell in love with. I fell in love with the complete person Kevin was. He was kind and loving and a man of few words, but when he loved and cared about you, he did it 110 percent, just like with his running. I could see in his pretty blue eyes how much he loved me. He treated me the way I saw my dad treat my mom. Often, he would leave me notes or send me cards expressing how he felt about me, us, and our future together. I did the same to him. I still have every note and card he gave me. We both knew we were lucky to have found each other and it was meant to be.

Today, when I hear that Mariah Carey song, it is bittersweet. It takes me back to that time in our lives when we were just beginning our relationship.

That first Christmas, Kevin gave me a crystal vase and promised to keep it full of flowers. He did just that until he died. I still have the vase, but since he has died, it has remained empty.

10

1996 Olympic Marathon Trials

The 1996 Olympic Marathon Trials were held in February in Columbia, South Carolina. The fall of 1994, after I had qualified, Harry (our mutual friend) and I took a road trip to Columbia, South Carolina, to view the course. We stayed with a host family. Stephanie and Pierce were so welcoming and kind. They helped with runners wanting to come to go over the course. They hooked me up with Rich and Mary-Ellen Kelly. Mary-Ellen had also qualified and was the hometown sweetheart. The qualifying time again was two hours and fifty minutes or faster.

Rich ran the first fifteen miles with me, and then Mary-Ellen ran the remainder of the course with me the next day. It was a challenging, hilly course, but I liked it. I preferred rolling courses to flat. From that moment, Mary-Ellen, Rich, and I became lifelong friends.

The trials arrived, and I flew down to Columbia while Kevin drove down with my friend Tammy's husband, Don. Tammy also had qualified for the trials. A lot of my family and friends came to support me, cheer me on, and share in the excitement of the whole event. Realistically, I knew I wasn't going to make the team, but I wanted to give it my all and enjoy the whole experience. I placed twenty-sixth overall out of over 129 runners and ran the course in two hours, forty minutes, and forty-nine seconds. The top three finishers made the Olympic team.

I got to meet some amazing other runners, hang out with Rich and Mary-Ellen, and cherish the moment. I will never forget being in the elevator with Willie Rios and Jenny Spangler, who won the trials along with some other runners he coached. Willie said to me, "Hey, you're the girl from *Runner's World.*" My Aunt Colleen had sent in a picture of me, telling them the story of how I had gone from running for the fun of it to qualifying. I thought it was funny how he remembered me from that tiny article.

That May, I decided to compete in the Pittsburgh Marathon. I placed second but learned that I would never run marathons that close to each other again. It took a toll on me, both mentally and physically. I ran the marathon in two hours, forty-three minutes, and two seconds. Two hours and forty-three minutes would be the time I could run on even the worst of days. Kevin ran in two hours, twenty-six minutes, and twenty-five seconds and placed fourteenth overall. Kevin's and my families were thrilled for the both of us, as we were for each other. After the race, I was so happy to see Kevin and hug him. Kevin always looked so handsome, but I really loved how he looked after running. He looked so cute all sweaty, and I loved his sweaty hugs.

A job opportunity came to me due to my placing second. A fellow runner and corporate officer from Bayer Corporation saw me on the news. He reached out to me and asked if I would be interested in a pharmaceutical sales position with the company. He felt I had all the right qualities to be a sales representative for them. Similar to sales, marathon training requires discipline, hard work, self-motivation, and setting/achieving goals. I told him yes, and thus, my pharmaceutical sales career began. As my career changed, so did the direction Coach Joe and I wanted to go with my running.

Joe and I decided to get outside help to hopefully get me to the next level. I remembered my conversation in the elevator with Willie; not only did he remember me from the article, but he also gave me his card in case I would want his help down the line. I contacted him with Joe's agreement. Willie wanted me to fly out to Santa Monica, California, where he could watch me run. Jenny Spangler was kind enough to let me stay at her place. Willie and I hit it off right away. I really liked him as a person and a possible coach. I loved how he believed in my potential. I was so excited by the prospect of Joe and me working with him. The plan would be to contact him once a week to get the workouts that I would do with Joe and tell Willie how the previous week's workouts went.

Willie had an interesting way of coaching. We would often have a long warm-up, then do a ton of two-hundreds followed by a long cool-down. He, along with Joe, got me in awesome shape. Willie, with Joe's agreement, wanted me to run the 1997 National Marathon Championship, which was also held in Columbia, South Carolina. The hope was to place in the top three and break two hours and forty minutes in order to make the US marathon team for the World Games in Athens, Greece.

As usual, the night before the marathon, I didn't sleep great, but I had my good-luck Santa my dad gave me. He bought it for me and told me it would be my good-luck charm. I made sure to always bring it with me to big races and sleep with it under my pillow the night before. Right before the race, I would rub it a couple of times for good luck (I have rubbed it so much over the years that its face has worn off). Then I would always warm up to "Dreams" by Van Halen, my inspirational song. I made sure Joe was at the start to help me relax. He would often tell me, "This is your stage. Show them what you are made of. All the hard work is done. Now is the time to enjoy the race." I know I drove him crazy at times wanting to go to the Porta-John just one more time. I remember, at a few races, him knocking on the door and telling me it was time to get to the start. (Now even when I am heading to one of my children's races and see a Porta-John, that runner in me gets nervous and feels like she has to go.)

At the start, I would get a good-luck hug from Joe, then do a few striders. Once on the line, I would check and recheck my shoelaces to make sure they were tied. When the national anthem played, I could feel my heart racing. All of this was just the nervous anticipation of the race. However, once the gun went off, I would settle in and let all the hard work and time I put in take over.

Sydney's good-luck Santa (left) and my good-luck Santa: gifts from my dad.

The day of the race was cold, rainy, and dreary. Willie had rubbed some Icy Hot on my lower back to help keep me warm throughout the race. I would see Willie and Joe along the course cheering me on. At mile twenty-one, I pushed hard up the hill and broke away from the runners with me. I vividly remember heading down the hill to the finish and Larry Grollman (the Pittsburgh Marathon race director at the time) screaming and cheering me on. I went on to place second and run the marathon in two hours, thirty-nine minutes, and eighteen seconds (my personal record), making the US marathon team for the World Championships in Greece. One of the nicest people I met through running, Mary Alico, also made the team.

US National Marathon Championship, Columbia, South Carolina – February 1997. From left: Julia Kirtland (won the race), me (placed second), and Mary Alico (placed third).

I was thrilled and, of course, so were Joe and Willie. But my two biggest fans, Kevin and my dad, were especially proud of me. Everyone agreed: this was a once-in-a-lifetime opportunity.

Winsome threesome: The top three of the US Women's Marathon championships—Julia Kirtland (left), Cheryl Collins (center), and Mary Alico (right)—celebrate at the awards ceremony. *Runner's World*, May 1997.

11

My Personal Life Was
Taking Off Too

After Kevin and I dated for a little over a year, he sat me down on the front steps of his house and asked if I would marry him and make this *our* home.

Of course, I cried and said yes. That is exactly what we went on to do: make it our home. We both knew early on that we wanted to spend the rest of our lives together and have a family together. He had everything I wanted in a life partner. I wanted to shout from the rooftops, "Kevin Gatons just asked me to be his wife," but instead, I called my twin sister, then my mom and dad to tell them the happy news. (Ironically, I called in the same order on November 3, 2006, but that time to share the devastating news.) Then, we went to Kevin's parents' house to tell them and show them the ring. Kevin picked out the ring all by himself. It was gorgeous. It had a thicker band because he wanted something sturdier for me in case I would fall running. He knew me too well, and yes, eventually I would trip a couple of times on sidewalks, uneven surfaces, or roots along a trail.

Today, my engagement ring, along with my wedding band, sit in a glass case. I kept them on for three years after Kevin died. It took a long time to accept I was no longer officially married since "death do us part" happened. Neither Kevin nor I chose to end our marriage. It ended with his dying and no longer could be the way we thought it would be. We never stopped loving each other and never will.

Finally, after three years, my emotional coach (one of the many therapists who helped me survive) convinced me it was time. I first moved the rings to my right hand and then eventually took them off.

I remember on one occasion, a man assumed I was divorced since I no longer had my wedding ring on. It was a pretty awful moment. The children and I were at a swimming pool the kids liked because it had a slide and high dives. A grown man kept yelling at my kids along with other kids to give him a chance to go down the slide. I said to him, "They are just kids." He responded in a mean voice, "No wonder you're divorced!" I then said, "I am not divorced—my husband died." I think for a brief moment I wanted him to feel bad, but when he apologized, I told him it was fine. In that instance, I—and I believe also he—learned to never assume you know what is going on in someone's life. I too realized it didn't matter what others thought. My taking my wedding ring off was just one more step forward in the healing process.

Over the years, I have had people suggest that I have my ring made into a necklace or something else. I would never alter it from its original form, for that ring symbolizes the love Kevin and I had and will always have. It is perfect as is. Initially it made me sad to look at, but now I can smile and remember a precious time in my life that I am grateful to have had.

To tell you the truth, I sometimes don't even remember what it's like to be married since I have been on my own longer then I was with Kevin. We only got to be married for eight years. When I allow myself to go there, I think about how I will never celebrate a tenth, twenty-fifth, or fiftieth wedding anniversary. That really saddens me, so I don't allow my mind to go there often.

After Kevin proposed, we immediately started making wedding plans. I was so excited to marry my Prince Charming. I wanted a fairytale wedding, a big church wedding with all our family and friends.

I loved being married and having a partner in life. Someday, I hope to have that again. I haven't given up on love over the last twelve years; I just had a more important priority, which was raising our children. They were extremely young when Kevin died, and they needed me more than ever. It also took a long time for me to be open to the idea of loving again. Through therapy, I realized that I am capable of loving another.

I was never a "dater" before I met Kevin, and the idea of going out to bars is just not me. Online dating would not be for me either. Friends have been kind and introduced me to friends of theirs, but none were right for me or my situation.

I did briefly date a man I met at a race. He was nothing like Kevin. At first, I thought this was a good thing—I wouldn't make comparisons. However, as time went on, I realized he was so wrong for me. The person I want to be with would need to be more like the kind of person Kevin was.

I'm okay on my own. I have resolved myself to the fact that if it is meant to be, it will be. I do feel that more than likely it will occur in the environment I am most comfortable in and myself— something having to do with running. I feel I fit in most among runners.

12
World Games

August of 1997 was the World Championships in Athens, Greece. I was so excited to be going as a member of the USA marathon team. What an honor and privilege it was to me.

I trained extremely hard with Joe under Willie's coaching. Joe and I met during his lunch hour and trained during the heat of the day to prepare for Greece, never really knowing at the time how much that would pay off on race day.

Joe always made the difficult speed workouts and long runs fun and easier by cracking some sort of joke. He also understood when it was time to shorten or change up a speed workout if I was no longer hitting the times. He knew as a coach it was better for my mental and physical well-being. On one of my last twenty-milers, we decided to bag it at mile twelve since I had nothing left and try again the following weekend. The following weekend, we regrouped, and I was able to run a good twenty-miler. Joe taught me it was just as important to listen to my mind and body as an athlete as it was to get the training in. Recovery is essential in being a competitive runner, especially a marathoner.

As the race approached, I flew from Pittsburgh, Pennsylvania, to La Guardia in New York, where I met up with Willie. Then we took the long flight to Athens, Greece. Joe would arrive later. My luggage got lost for a few days, but fortunately, I had my racing flats and gear in my carry-on.

I remember Gwen Coogan (an amazing runner) being so kind and saying I could borrow her clothes. I said, "But you are so tiny," and she laughed and said, "So are you." Eventually, my luggage did arrive.

I wanted to experience and take in every moment, since I knew how lucky I was to be there representing the USA. I went to several track and field events and went sightseeing with some of the other athletes, creating wonderful memories

Marathon day came. I, along with the rest of the USA team and the runners from other countries, boarded a bus extremely early in the morning to head to the 7:00 a.m. race start. The race started early in hopes of avoiding the extreme heat of Athens. It was the original marathon course, which started out in the country in the battlefield of the small town of Marathon, which is on the coast, and finished in the original Olympic stadium in Athens, Greece.

The weather was not ideal to run 26.2 miles. At 7:00 a.m., it was already ninety-seven degrees and 100 percent humidity. My goal was to finish despite the conditions and to do the best I could representing the USA.

I remember, like it was yesterday, hitting the wall at mile eleven. My legs went to rubber due to the extreme heat. This had never happened to me before, let alone with 15.2 miles to go. It was the World Championships, and I wasn't going to drop no matter what. *No quitting*, I told myself. I focused by staying on the blue line painted on the road and envisioned Joe waiting in the Olympic Stadium, pulling me in. Joe was the kind of coach who you wanted to run hard for. He always wanted me to run hard for myself, but there were moments that I ran for him as well. This was one of them. Unfortunately, a lot of runners around me were dropping out due to the heat. It was a grueling 26.2 miles, but at the same time, running the original marathon course meant so much. I was running a part of history, so I dug in.

As I entered the Olympic Stadium, I saw Joe running back and forth, screaming with joy as if I had won the race. I placed twenty-fifth in the world, was the top American, and was just so happy to have been able to finish. Many runners required IV solutions after the race due to the extreme conditions. Fortunately, I didn't; I ran the marathon in two hours, forty-three minutes, and forty-two seconds. I knew going into it that Willie and Joe had gotten me into the best shape of my life, and I probably would have run faster, but the conditions didn't allow for me getting a personal record. Running well is not always about time, but about determination, persistence, and belief. Joe, Willie, Kevin, my family, and my friends were so happy for me.

Coach Joe Sarver and me after the World Championship marathon race inside the original Olympic Stadium - Athens, Greece, 1997.

One of my dad's proudest moments was when he saw my name on TV as the top American finisher. He used to say to me, "Cheryl, I don't like to drive 26.2 miles. How do you run 26.2 miles?" As any marathoner knows, you get used to it from your training, but there are some races where you really have to dig deep into yourself. I felt that is what I did in Athens.

Before I headed home, I watched the men's race and attended the closing ceremonies with some of the other athletes. It was amazing to be on the field dancing and singing with athletes from all over the world. I will never forget that moment where I experienced a feeling of oneness with the world.

13
The Next Step

After the world games, Joe and I decided to seek outside help from another coach. Willie helped me get into the best shape of my life, and I will be forever grateful for that, but we didn't see eye to eye on running being my whole life. I was never only a runner. I didn't start competitive running until the age of twenty-eight. I was never going to *only* be a runner.

That fall, after the world games, I went to run the Tuff's 10K. Robert Sevene (Sev, as everyone calls him) agreed to come and watch me run in order to decide if he could coach me from afar while Joe acted as his eyes.

Coach Sev.

I had heard of Sev from some of my running friends, Mimi and Julie, who were being coached by him. After the race, I met Sev. He was a tall, athletic-looking man. You could tell he had been running his whole life. He made me feel comfortable in his presence despite all of his accolades. He was modest and only interested in my running. He told me that I ran very efficiently and was light on my feet. He said that as long as Joe was his eyes and we reported how the workouts went, he would coach me from afar.

So, every Sunday, I would call Sev and tell him how the past week's workouts went with Joe, and based on how they'd gone, he would give me the next week's workouts. The goal was to qualify again in the marathon for the 2000 Olympic Trials.

Sev's style of training was different then Willie's. Each week usually consisted of a long run anywhere from fifteen to twenty-two miles, a speed workout, and a PMP (preferred marathon pace, the pace I would run at the marathon) run. I would average eighty to eighty-five miles per week and sometimes do two-a-days to get the mileage in. Under Willie's coaching, I remember one time running one hundred miles in a week and realized it was just too much. Eighty to eighty-five miles per week was the max I could do without getting mentally and physically fatigued. Without breaking down as a runner. When you train at a high level, you walk a fine line between being healthy and getting injured. As a runner, the ultimate goal is to get to the starting line healthy and peaking at the right time. It also was the ultimate goal for Sev and Joe, as my coaches.

As I trained for Grandma's Marathon, which is held in June in Duluth, Minnesota, my wedding plans with Kevin were well on their way. The date picked was August 8, 1998. That was one of the reasons I had chosen to try to qualify at Grandma's Marathon. It would be behind me come our wedding day. Once we had the church and country club picked out, things really started to fall into place.

The wedding party, the invitations, the menu, and, of course, the wedding dress, the bridesmaids, etc., were all coming together.

Training was going well, and Joe and I really enjoyed Sev's coaching and help. Sev and I immediately hit it off. He, like Joe, coached for the right reasons. He wanted to help me succeed and reach my running goals by coaching me to my fullest potential. He cared about me not only as an athlete but as a person as well. I could talk to him about anything, just like with Joe. Another lifelong bond was formed.

Prior to Grandma's, I was given an amazing opportunity. Kathrine Switzer, the first woman to run the Boston Marathon as a numbered entry, had asked me to come to New York for the re-launching of the Avon race series. I was fortunate to have met and befriended Kathrine when she came to commentate the Pittsburgh Marathon. She and I even ran along the river during one of her visits. I really enjoyed her company. She is an amazing woman who is not only courageous, but also kind, genuine, and such a positive role model for women. I respected her and looked up to her for how much she did for women in the world of running and then some. If it weren't for her determination that day in Boston, I never would have had the running opportunities I had. She paved the way for so many of us.

Kathrine asked me, along with some of the most amazing female athletes, to come to the press launch in New York City. She wanted me to represent the up-and-coming runner while the likes of Joan Benoit Samuelson, Jackie Joyner-Kersee, and Lynn Jennings represented the already incredibly successful stars. Getting to meet the likes of Joan Benoit Samuelson and Jackie Joyner-Kersee, who were both Olympic gold medalists, was a lifetime memory.

The experience was so much fun, and to be among these iconic women was inspiring and special. We all headed to Central Park for a group photo and then back to the hotel for the reception announcing the new Avon race series. Kathrine had created Avon's first series, which ran from 1978 through 1985, and this led to getting the women's marathon event included in the Olympic Games and World Championships. I had been the happy recipient of her work in Athens. Now, after an eleven-year hiatus, Avon and Kathrine both were back to give women further global running opportunities. I was excited to be a part of it.

Avon Race Series. Standing, from left: Lorraine Moller, Joan Benoit Samuelson, Cheryl Collins, Martha Cooksey, Joyce Smith, Yuko Arimori. Sitting, from left: Nancy Conz, Lynn Jennings, Grete Waitz, Valentina Yegorova. *Runner's World*, December 1997.

At my table that afternoon was a woman from *Self* magazine. She had taken an interest in my story about trying to qualify for the Olympics/World Championships while getting married. From that conversation, I ended up flying back to New York for a photo shoot for *Self* magazine. They gave me a makeover and did wonderful photos of me in both running clothes and a wedding gown. It was a blast;

I felt like a model for a day and cherished this unexpected experience that had come from my running. It was a once-in-a-lifetime experience that I owe all to Kathrine Switzer. (Thank you, Kathrine!) Kathrine truly is one of the nicest and most amazing people I have met through my running. I will always treasure getting to know her and her influence on me and women's running.

To this day, Kathrine continues to push women forward and empower them through running. She is the founder of 261 Fearless, a global nonprofit organization which allows women to find strength, power, and fearlessness through running. 261 is the bib number she wore in the 1967 Boston Marathon, the day she became the pioneer for women runners and changed the world of running for women. Her being fearless on that day in Boston allowed me and so many before and after me to be all they could be in the world of running. Kathrine always says, "Running will wonderfully change your life. Let it." On that day in Boston, it changed the path her life would take along with so many others'.

A treasured note from Kathrine Switzer.

Boston Herald, 1967 - Kathrine Switzer making history as the first woman to officially run the Boston Marathon and getting attacked by a race official for doing so. With the help of her teammates, she finished the race.

2017 – Fifty years after her first legendary run in Boston, Kathrine does it again to celebrate women's huge running accomplishments. She is in the middle with the baseball cap on. (Photo courtesy of Kathrine Switzer.)

Self Magazine. June 1998. Fiorenzo Borghi. Photographer.

June came, and Julie, Mimi, and I headed to Grandma's Marathon in hopes of qualifying. Ironically, Grandma's was Kevin's favorite marathon. He reached a personal record there with two hours and twenty-four minutes.

GRANDMA'S MARATHON
June 17, 1995

Once at Grandma's, Julie, Mimi, and I all qualified for the 2000 Olympic marathon trials. I finished in two hours, thirty-nine minutes, and thirty-seven seconds. I qualified for the A standard for the trials, which meant I would get my flight along with my room paid for. Kevin loved that course since he had gotten a personal record there. It was an extremely well-run race. The course was a great course to achieve a personal record on, but I didn't like the course as much as Kevin did.

You were taken out 26.2 miles and basically ran straight back in along Lake Superior, which was beautiful. I prefer courses that have turns and a change of scenery. I liked courses that were rolling versus flat since I ran well on hills. I also liked using different muscles throughout the race. It made the marathon mentally and physically easier for me. On a rolling course, I was always told by my coaches to maintain the same effort throughout the race. Hills and downhills allowed for recovery and mixing things up. Grandma's wasn't completely flat—it had some gently rolling hills—but it was its point-to-point course that bothered me mentally. Plus, it was extremely foggy that day along the lake, and you could barely see the balloon markers in the distance for each mile.

I remember running most of the race with a woman from Canada who was hoping to qualify for the Canadian Olympic trials. Running with her made the straight course mentally easier for me to run. We truly helped each other, and both of us went on to qualify. We thanked each other. Through running, I have had the opportunity to meet some of the nicest people, and for 26.2 miles, my Canadian friend was one of them.

14
New Partner in Life and in Training

Our wedding day was August 8, 1998. It felt like a fairytale. I was the princess about to ride off with her prince. I was thirty-two years old and had waited my whole life to find someone like Kevin. It was everything I imagined as a little girl.

We got married at Sacred Heart Church in Shadyside, Pennsylvania. It is a beautiful old church. I had belonged to it when I lived in Shadyside right out of college before moving to California. The ceremony was gorgeous, despite the church being hot. Walking down the aisle on my dad's arm and then being handed off to Kevin was more than I could have ever dreamed of. They were the two most important men in my life. I was blessed.

When the priest said, "'til death do us part," I never imagined it would come so soon. Nor did I ever imagine that I would lose the two most important men in my life back to back.

At the reception, Kevin and I did our first dance to Frank Sinatra's "For Once in My Life." We chose this song because I felt it had taken me forever to find Kevin, while Kevin, at one point, despite his having had a previous serious relationship, thought he would never find the right person to marry. So, it was perfect for us. We even took ballroom dance lessons to prepare. Kevin dipped me at the end and kissed me. The wedding was perfect in every way. (If only life could be perfect in every way.) To be Mrs. Kevin Gatons was a dream come true.

I'm so happy that runner noticed me at the races. Meeting Kevin truly was and still is the best thing to come out of my running.

We had begun our life together. We were so excited about what laid ahead, never knowing how short our time together would be, never knowing, even at that happy moment, that Kevin had an underlying heart condition that would rob us of ever growing old together. Not the lifetime of love we both wanted. Kevin, on our wedding video, promised me a lifetime of love. He did do that (his lifetime), but I wanted it for longer. I do have to believe he forever loves me and the children from afar.

Once Kevin and I were married, I would do most of my speed workouts with him since it was easier than driving an hour to meet Joe. I still met Joe on occasion, and I would always report the workouts to Joe and Sev.

I was spoiled. I had Joe and now Kevin pacing me. It made my work easier and mindless. I would just stay right with them. They would hit the pace exactly. I wasn't good at pacing. If I needed to do five-minute-twenty-second-mile repeats, every two hundred would be forty seconds and the quarters would be eighty. They were like human pace machines. In the early stages of my training, I hated the track. I didn't have a track background, and I found it boring. Joe would have me do my workouts with him on marked trails, markers he measured on the road or the mall parking lot. I despised the track, and this method was mentally easier for me to do.

Eventually, Joe convinced me the track was my friend since it was exact. Joe and Kevin made the workouts effortless for me. I just sat on them.

Joe and Kevin had known each other long before I had met either of them. They were teammates on Allegheny Nike (a local Pittsburgh running club), and they were also fierce competitors at one time. Joe completely understood when I started to do them with Kevin. It made sense with regards to time and convenience. I really did love training with Kevin too. The only difference was that on occasion (Kevin might have said more), I would complain to him to slow down or pick it up, which I never did with Joe. My dad once said that Joe was the only person I always listened to. Joe also told me I was a great athlete to coach since I always listened, not like the girl running for the social aspect back in high school. That's probably why I ended up having as much success as I did. I complained to Kevin because he was my husband and I knew I could. I especially did it when I was tired. My feeling comfortable and being so close to Kevin allowed me to be "bratty" on occasion.

I will never forget the one time when we were doing five-minute-twenty-second-mile repeats on the track and it was extremely hot. I kept complaining to him to either slow down or pick it up. Finally, in the middle of one of the mile repeats, Kevin came to a dead stop, threw his arms in the air, and said, "I'm done." I apologized; we continued the workout, and I kept my mouth shut.

Joe and Kevin made me a faster and stronger runner since they both were faster than me. Kevin used to joke that the moment I started beating him (he was six years older), he was going to quit competing. I don't think that would have happened. His marathon personal record was two hours and twenty-four minutes, and Joe's is two hours, twenty minutes, and thirty seconds.

I found out from Joe after Kevin died that he had sent Joe a card thanking him for coaching "his bratty wife" for all those years. That made me cry. Yes, I was "bratty" a few times with Kevin. I recall a ten-mile PMP run I was doing with him with less than two miles to go. I fell down in the grass along the road. He looked at me as if he were thinking, *What the hell just happened?* I looked back at him and said, "I can't finish." I think at first, he thought I was being dramatic, but then he realized I was really done. We walked the rest of the way home.

Another time was during one of my twenty-milers. I would usually hide a bottle with my marathon drink, diluted grape Gatorade, and a Gu (an energy gel) out on the course, but on occasion, Kevin would drive and meet me somewhere along the way. It was an extremely hot day. I kept looking for Kevin. I was so thirsty that even puddles were looking good. I stopped at a fire station, and they were kind enough to give me a cup of water. I drank it as I continued to run. Finally, I saw Kevin's truck. He said, "Sorry, I didn't think you would be so fast." I looked at him and said, "Thanks, but never mind," and ran the rest of the way home.

Yes, "bratty" would be the kind word to describe me in those moments. Kevin was and always will be my favorite training partner and person to run with, but Joe definitely is a close second. I was blessed to have them both to train with. They always were willing to do my specific workouts, whether it was for a 5K, 10K, half marathon, or marathon, to help me without worrying about their own running. They made me so much better.

Some of my personal records are as follows:

5K – 16:55 (Brentwood Firecracker, Brentwood, PA)

10K – 33:29 (The Great Race in Pittsburgh, PA)

Half Marathon – 1:15:33 (Motorola Half Marathon, Chicago, IL)

25K – 1:30:17 (Old Kent River Bank Run, MI)

Marathon – 2:39:18 (National Championship in Columbia, SC)

I would have never run those times without Joe and Kevin helping me, along with Joe's, Sev's, and Willie's coaching. I also never would have placed second twice in the Pittsburgh Marathon, second at the National Marathon Championship, and second at the Harrisburg Marathon without their help and support. I too would never have captured my first marathon win at the 2018 Johnstown Marathon!

> For the Greensburg runner—and Pitt-Johnstown graduate—the Johnstown victory was the culmination of a "lifetime" of running that started when she was an electrical engineering major at the Richland Township campus from 1985 to 1989. "I've never won one. When I was competitive, I never ran a low-key one, so I thought I'm gonna run one and try to win." She was also happy to point out that her win came close to where her running odyssey began. "My love for running started at UPJ when I was in college," Collins-Gatons said. "To have my last marathon here is pretty good."

(Courtesy of Shawn Curtis, sports editor of *The Tribune-Democrat*)

I feel that with my win at the Johnstown Marathon, my running had come full circle.

15
Sydney, Australia

The 2000 Olympics were to be held in Sydney, Australia. I had qualified for the trials, which were going to be held in Columbia, South Carolina, again. The plan was to run the trials and then start a family since I was going to be thirty-four and Kevin would be forty.

I ran the trials that morning and placed twenty-seventh in two hours, forty-six minutes, and eleven seconds. We wasted no time and actually conceived that night in Columbia. Neither of us thought it would happen so quickly. Once I found out I was pregnant, we decided that, regardless if the baby were a boy or a girl, he or she would be named Sidney or Sydney. That baby was so meant to be. I just felt it.

Kevin always found out the sex of the baby with each pregnancy, while I wanted to be surprised. He was very good at keeping secrets. I was able to run my whole pregnancy, even on the day I delivered. I looked like I had a basketball in my belly.

Sydney was three weeks early. I remember waking up and leaking a little. I mentioned it to Kevin, but neither of us thought much about it. He headed to school, and I went for my run. I came back drenched. My leggings were soaked. My water had broken. I called my doctors, and they told me to head to the hospital. I then called Kevin and told him I was going to the hospital and I would update him. With it being our first baby, neither of us realized you had to deliver once your water broke. Eventually, Kevin joined me at the hospital, and we welcomed our first child into the world—a healthy baby girl who cried as she entered the world and who made us both cry tears of joy. The love between the three of us was immediate.

I did attempt to qualify one more time for the trials. The plans were to run the New York Marathon and hope to qualify, and then celebrate Sydney's first birthday. Training was different this time. Not the workouts, per se, and I still cared, but I cared more about being a mom. I remember one time when Kevin and I ran with Sydney in the baby jogger to the track to do a workout. We placed the stroller on the field and gave Sydney a toy to play with. Every time we ran by her, she would cry. That really bothered both Kevin and me. From then on, his mom would come and watch Sydney while we did the workout.

New York was the first qualifier. 9/11 occurred, and there was talk of canceling the marathon. I had been an invited runner, and I have to say it was a sad, patriotic, and overwhelming experience. I will never forget being in the elite holding area and seeing Mayor Rudy Giuliani being helicoptered in to start the race. Security was extremely tight. I ran with an American flag on my shirt, and so did many others. The crowd support was outstanding, and it made us all feel united. There was more meaning in those 26.2 miles than qualifying. Those miles defined how strong New York was and how united the world could be. It was definitely one of my favorite and most memorable marathons, despite my missing qualifying by a couple of minutes (two hours, fifty-one minutes, ten seconds). It was time to hang up my racing shoes and focus on growing our family.

Quintin was our next child to be delivered. Once again, I ran my entire pregnancy, most of the time while pushing Sydney in the baby jogger. All my children would love the baby jogger. My delivery again was extremely quick and easy. Kevin named Quintin after his favorite character, Quenton Cassidy, in the book *Once a Runner* by

John L. Parker Jr. As stated in *Once a Runner* in regards to the character Quenton Cassidy, "Running to him was real, the way he did it the realest thing he knew. It was all joy and woe, hard as diamond; it made him weary beyond comprehension. But it also made him free. . . . " Running made Kevin feel free, and it does the same for me.

As our family grew, I would still compete at the annual Fourth of July race. Kevin helped out with the race, which benefited the American Heart Association. (The irony of life. We had no idea Kevin had an underlying heart condition.) I would go on to win that race each year and then go back to running for the fun of it, just like I used to do.

Kevin. Freedom 5K. Greensburg. Pennsylvania - July 2006. four months before he died. One of my favorite running photos of Kevin.

As the family grew, Kevin and I didn't get to run together as much. Often, he would run first, then I would run, or if that couldn't happen, I would push Sydney and Quintin in the double baby jogger. Kevin, being older, was okay with having a healthy girl and boy. I wanted more, but we weren't really planning on it. Then Lillian happened. We were both thrilled to add her to our family. I often call her my gift from God since she was so young when Kevin died that I had no choice but to survive.

Kevin continued to run for fitness and, on occasion, raced here and there. He still was very competitive, so when he qualified for the Boston Marathon, he was thrilled. He ran Boston in April of 2006, just six months before he died. That would be his last marathon and the last time Joe Sarver would see Kevin. Joe had also qualified and was running when Kevin noticed Joe ahead and came upon him and said, "Hey, Sarver."

Joe, like Kevin, had a distinct running form that was easy to notice. Kevin ran with his hands in a fist going downward and Joe with his head tilted to the side (bobbing side to side). I could spot both of them anywhere. On that day, though, Kevin had spotted Joe out of thousands of runners. Joe and Kevin ran together for quite a while. Then Kevin told him to go ahead. He was struggling a little. When Joe said goodbye and went on, he never thought it would be goodbye forever.

It really bothered Joe after Kevin had passed that he didn't run a little longer with him. Kevin was having a bad race for him, and he just chalked it up to not training properly since he was so busy with teaching, coaching, going back to school, taking care of rentals, and, most especially, taking care of his family. He had no idea in that moment how bad his heart already was. I thank God all the time that he didn't die there. It might have been even more horrific if it had happened there. I would have been mad at him for running Boston, thinking it was a heart attack. God still had more for Kevin to do.

Since we didn't get to run together that often anymore, when we did, it was special. Our common bond, our common love of running is what brought us together in the first place.

A month before Kevin died, we got to run our favorite loop in Schenley Park together, a trail park in Pittsburgh. I can still picture our last run together and will forever treasure that run. At first it was hard for me to go back there and run after Kevin died, but now when I run there, I feel close to him. I can vividly see him running a golf glove he found down to some young golfers and then running up the hill to meet me on the other side. Every time I run by that spot, I think of that moment. There were times after Kevin died when I wished we could have stayed in that moment . . . frozen forever . . . just the two of us running endlessly on the trails . . . never stopping.

16
Life Was Good

We had it all. Three healthy, beautiful children, and we were each other's best friend. Kevin and I loved being with each other and our children. Once Kevin and I found out we were pregnant with Lilly, we decided it would be for the best if I stayed home with the children. I had continued to work as a pharmaceutical sales representative with Sydney and Quintin. They would go to daycare three days a week, and Kevin's mom would watch them the other two days. With our growing family, we felt it was time for me to stay home. Life was simple, but we had everything we ever dreamed of. Life was good. Kevin often said out loud, "I love my life." I, too, loved my life back then. It was how I grew up believing my life would be. We made good choices, and so far, everything had gone according to the plan (our plan, not necessarily God's).

As our children were growing, Kevin was busy teaching, coaching, and going back to school to become a principal, but he always made the four of us his priority. We were his life. He always made time for our children and me. He was an amazing dad, taking them to parks, playing with them, reading to them, buying them clothes, and loving them all the time. Just like he did the moment they came into the world. With each one, Kevin cried, held them tight, and loved them instantly. He was a great husband, too, always there for me no matter what.

Kevin was my biggest fan in life and especially running, just like my dad. I will never forget my dad saying to me that he had been at Mitsubishi Electric in Cranberry and noticed a race brochure. He opened it up and saw that, after all these years, I still held the course record. That made him smile. It was the Thornhill 5K. If you broke seventeen minutes, you got additional prize money. I asked Mark Courtney, a fellow runner, if he could pace me to break seventeen minutes. He agreed to, and with his help, I did just that. I ran the course in sixteen minutes and fifty-six seconds, winning the women's race and breaking the course record.

My dad was not only my biggest fan, but he also acted like a concerned dad in regards to my running. When I first moved home, he went out and bought me a treadmill because he didn't want me running on icy/snow-covered roads in the dark. He was relieved when I started wearing reflectors to run at five in the morning on dark country roads. A woman who passed me each morning on her way to work gave them to me. She was worried that I might get hit. Her kind gesture was appreciated by me but most especially by my parents, who were also concerned I might get hit by a car.

Kevin and my dad were so excited when I got a letter saying I was going to be inducted into my high school hall of fame. They were thrilled at my achievement. I was the luckiest girl in the world. I grew up with an awesome, supportive dad, and now I had a wonderful husband and father to our children. Of course, like any marriage, there were moments that Kevin and I might have disagreed on something, but we always talked it out. That's what best friends do.

Kevin often said that he loved how I could sweat with the best of them and still get dressed up and look nice. He fell in love first with the sweaty runner. I loved spending time with Kevin and our children. We were a family, and Kevin and I loved that. We were happy and knew how lucky we were to have each other.

Like me as a little girl, our children would be so excited when Daddy got home. They loved him. He was an incredible dad. I, too, loved when he would come home. I can picture him walking in the door after coaching in his running clothes, carrying his gym bag with his tie draped around his neck (he didn't want his tie to get wrinkled once he took it off the hook in his truck). The children would usually get to him first and hug him; then it was my turn. How I would give anything for Kevin to walk through the front door and hug all of us.

I will never forget when we took Sydney to see *The Polar Express* movie. He then went out and bought the book for Sydney and wrote inside it, "May you forever hear the sweet sound of the bell. Merry Christmas and Love Always, Mom and Dad." That sums up what kind of dad he was. Sydney still has that book and will forever know that her dad loved her. That is one thing our children will always have: their dad's love in their hearts. They know he held them, loved them, and would have never chosen to leave. It wasn't his choice on November 3, 2006, to leave the children and me behind. He didn't abandon us. He had no choice. It wasn't our plan. It was God's plan.

A special gift Sydney will always treasure.

Christmas 2005 - One year before our lives changed forever.

17
November 3, 2006

November 3, 2006, was the most horrific day of my life. How could a day start out so normally and end so horribly?

As the children and I were heading to an evening of fun, Kevin was navigating the Hershey State Cross Country course with Samantha Bower and Noelle Blank. Kevin coached Samantha, and she had qualified for the state cross country race the next day. He was showing her the course like he always did with his athletes before races. Things were going normally; he was talking strategy to Samantha, laughing, and being a supportive coach. They had just passed Coach Rich Wright, the Baldwin High School coach. Kevin said, "Hi," and wished him and his athlete good luck tomorrow. Once at the top of the hill, it seemed as if Kevin had tripped and fell. Samantha, at first, thought he was joking with her (he would do something like that). I remember on one of my runs with Samantha her telling me everything about that day prior to that moment. She told me what he ate and how he behaved, and nothing seemed out of sorts with Kevin until then.

Suddenly, Coach Wright knew Kevin hadn't tripped by Samantha's reaction. Once she knew Kevin wasn't joking, panic overcame her. Coach Wright ran to Kevin and immediately had another runner call nine-one-one as he started CPR and told Samantha, Noelle, and the girl running with him to leave and get help. Coach Wright performed CPR as he talked to Kevin. He told me that he told Kevin to hang on for Cheryl and the children, never knowing there was no hope in saving Kevin.

Left to right: Samantha Bower, Noelle Blank, Jeremy Lenzi, and Kevin. Dick's Sporting Goods Year in Review: In Memoriam – December 2006.

See, his heart had been enlarged and damaged all over, as if he'd had several heart attacks. There was no good conductive tissue left. I found all this out later. He must have been having arrhythmias that he wasn't aware of because on that day, he went into v-fib (ventricular fibrillation—a life-threatening heart rhythm). I did later find out from Samantha that he had actually stopped a mile in for no apparent reason and then started running again. Samantha said she never thought anything of that because he continued to coach her; she figured he probably thought whatever he felt in that moment was nothing. I have often wondered if he had never run another step after he had briefly stopped, would he still be here? The doctors tell me no because it was inevitable. So, in a single heartbeat, all that I believed and knew about life was taken away. I thought if you were a good person and made good choices, life worked out. Kevin was a good person and made good choices.

I will never forget Coach Rich Wright saying to me later, "How could someone be so full of life in one moment and then gone the next?" I will be forever grateful for Coach Wright being there for Kevin when he really needed someone the most. The children and I had thought about going to the race, but they always wanted Daddy to carry them or play with them. I felt it wouldn't be fair to Samantha. Kevin wanted to be able to focus on Samantha's race. Thank God we weren't there. I have found peace in the fact Kevin was doing two of the things he loved the most: coaching and running. Plus, he had no idea of what was to come.

Knowing he got immediate help brings me comfort too. I was told even if Kevin had fallen outside of a hospital, there was no saving him. His heart was too far gone. If, by chance, he had survived, he would have needed a heart transplant and become completely sedentary. That in itself might have killed Kevin. Taking the runner in him away would have changed the Kevin I knew and loved.

How could someone act so normal and seem so healthy on the outside while slowly dying on the inside? To think I was concerned about a mole he had on his chest, never thinking that the real concern was the heart beating inside his chest.

Another blessing in the way Kevin died was that he wasn't alone, and I didn't have to go and find him somewhere lying alone after one of his morning runs. Thank God he didn't hurt anyone while driving or have this happen while driving our children. God gave Kevin the perfect way to die, only forty-some years too early.

18
ARVD (a.k.a. ARVC)

Initially, after Kevin died, everyone automatically assumed he'd had a heart attack; that was the rumor around town. I wasn't so willing to accept that answer. Yes, I understand it could have been the case, but my first instinct was to dig deeper. So, I kept calling the coroner's office in Dauphin County in the hopes of getting some answers. Answers to explain how this could be. Finally, a pathologist said to me, "I really think he had ARVD." To give me peace of mind, he asked if he could have the heart sent to Texas to be studied by Dr. Marcus, who first described the disease in the early 1980s.

ARVD means Arrhythmogenic Right Ventricular Dysplasia. It is also known as ARVC or Arrhythmogenic Right Ventricular Cardiomyopathy. What exactly does that mean? Until Kevin's untimely passing, I had never heard of it. It's a rare genetic disorder affecting the heart's muscle that wasn't discovered until the 1980s (so it's a relatively new disease).

This disorder is a result of a genetic mutation, which is exasperated by athleticism or intense exercising (aerobic activity). This genetic mutation affects the heart in ways that alter its normal function and structure. The right side of the heart is often enlarged with reduced function. Individuals with ARVD often have an abnormal electrocardiogram or EKG as well as frequent PVCs or extra beats.

As the heart enlarges to compensate for the increased strain, it becomes damaged due to fat and scar replacing good heart cells.

Quite often, young athletes die suddenly from this disorder, just like Kevin did on November 3, 2006, because they didn't know they were at increased risk of having a life-threatening arrhythmia. Kevin lived longer than most who aren't treated for this disease. The symptoms are so slight that often they go undetected. The symptoms are lightheadedness, dizziness, and a rapid heartbeat. Often, they go unnoticed or are mistaken for dehydration, fatigue, or even hypothermia. If Kevin would have gone to a doctor complaining of dizziness, it more than likely would have been labeled as something else. If he was given an EKG, it probably would also have gone undetected since it is extremely difficult to diagnose. There is no single test that can diagnosis ARVD. The diagnosis is made by analyzing results from several cardiac tests that assess the structure and function of the heart.

If, by chance, we would have known Kevin had ARVD early on, he would have had to live with a defibrillator in his heart and not participate in competitive athletics. This would have meant no more running. He would have had to live a more sedentary life. Yes, he would have probably done this to be here with his children and me, but like I stated earlier, he wouldn't have been the same person. However, his heart was so damaged that a defibrillator probably wouldn't have worked and his only option would have been a transplant.

ARVD is a cause of sudden death. Unfortunately, the first sign of the disease can be sudden death. Kevin never even got a chance to be treated; however, if our children, God forbid, should have it, they can be treated properly and lead a life without strenuous exercise. Despite Kevin and I both being serious runners, I know he would agree with me that it's a sacrifice worth living with. Our children, their spouses, their children, and their spouses will never have to go through what I, our children, his family, my family, and our friends went through on November 3, 2006. I would never wish that on anyone.

It was a good thing that I was so persistent in not accepting a heart attack as the cause of death. The study went on to find Kevin did have ARVD, and since ARVD runs in families, our children could also have it. Thank goodness I know the true answer, we know what we are looking for, and the children can get screened regularly for signs of ARVD. Thank you to Dr. Wayne Ross of Harrisburg, Pennsylvania, for listening to my cries of confusion and not thinking I was crazy for calling over and over again in search of answers to understand how Kevin died. Because he understood my need for answers and his actions that followed, I found the answer I needed and our children can be tested. I knew deep down inside it was more than a heart attack.

There is hope and promise that a person with ARVD can lead a fulfilling life. Kevin led a fulfilling life and achieved more than the average athlete despite this disorder. The doctors told me that it is amazing that he did all he did and didn't die sooner. It is such an irony that when Kevin was running in hopes of staying young for his children, this disorder was actually being brought out. It is often referred to as the "backward heart disease," for when you think you are doing something good for the heart, you are actually damaging the heart. If Kevin had never run or played basketball or baseball, he would more than likely still be here, but ARVD didn't define Kevin—his athleticism did. It was who he was meant to be regardless of the disease.

The summer before Kevin died, he was running with friends and stopped suddenly, kind of like on November 3 with Samantha. They asked what was wrong, and he said he felt a little lightheaded. They asked if this had ever happened before, and he said it had a long time ago. I never knew of this incident until after Kevin had died. Like most runners, he assumed it was nothing.

If our children do have ARVD, we will cross that bridge when the time comes. In the meantime, they live as normal, healthy children and play lots of sports. A few summers ago, while we were waiting for Dr. Crosson to tell us the results from the testing (the testing right now is to get baseline cardiac tests to compare to when they are more in their teen years since that is when it starts to become present), my son, Quintin, who looks just like his dad and loves all sports, said he would rather die than give up sports. This probably is something his dad would have said as a young boy, too. He is so competitive and intense like his father. He was three when Kevin died. His mannerisms, etc., are so his dad. It truly must be innate.

We will continue to go to Johns Hopkins every three years until they reach their late thirties. I pray that it was a one-time fluke and our children don't have it. Thank goodness we know what to look for and know that they can live with it.

If anyone you know might have symptoms of ARVD, go to www.arvd.com or please contact:

Crystal Tichnell, MGC
Genetic Counselor / Program Coordinator
Johns Hopkins Hospital
600 North Wolfe Street, Blalock 545
Baltimore, Maryland 21287
Phone: 410-502-7161 Fax: 410-502-9148
Email: ctichnel@jhmi.edu

A special note of thanks to Crystal for her collaboration with me in writing this chapter.

19
My New Reality

The day after the funeral, reality started to set in. This was my new life, a life without Kevin. How was I going to survive this horrible heartache and raise three children without having them grow up dysfunctional or for their lives to be forever dictated by their father's dying? I wasn't sure if I could keep my head above water, let alone three other little lives who really needed me. The pain was unbearable. I can't even explain how badly my heart hurt and how grief-stricken I was. I guess my face said it all. My eyes no longer sparkled. I had a blank, lifeless stare.

Our family was no longer complete. I was afraid of being alone with just the children. Something/someone was obviously missing. There was an emptiness. I only felt safe being around or talking to certain people. I didn't have the energy, and I was sad.

Initially, there was a flood of visitors, endless flowers, and sympathy cards. I hated it all, even though everyone meant well. It just reconfirmed my new reality.

On November 9, 2006, one day after I buried Kevin, I was to be inducted into my high school hall of fame (Plum High) for my running accomplishments. At first, when I received the news prior to Kevin's dying, I thought what a great way to celebrate turning forty with Kevin, our children, and my family, never knowing that I would be spending my fortieth birthday (November 8) in the cemetery burying my husband. I thought I still might be able to attend, but I realized I was depleted and no way in a mood to celebrate. My dad's back was hurting, so he wasn't up for it either. Without my two biggest fans and most important men in my life there, it wouldn't be the same. I asked them to delay my induction by a year, and they agreed to honor my request. I would go in with the 2007 inductees, and maybe by then, I would be up for it.

The following year, I went on to get inducted surrounded by my mom, siblings, daughter Sydney (since she was old enough to attend), and my coach Joe, and his wife, Judy. My two biggest fans were missing, but I do believe they were smiling and cheering me on.

It is so hard to explain grief unless you have gone through it. The grief I experienced losing Kevin versus my grandparents was completely different. It was debilitating. With my grandparents, I knew eventually it would happen with them being older, but with my young husband, the grief overtook every waking moment. From the moment I woke up until I went to bed, I could not escape the devastation of the grief I was feeling. It consumed every ounce of my energy and my body. I went from a happy, high-energy young woman to a depressed individual who could hardly get out of bed. I could not recognize myself. I woke up wanting the day to be over already, and instead, it lasted forever, endlessly, day after day. I was not really alive; I was just trying to survive.

I also remember so many people, people I didn't even know well, wanting to help. It was overwhelming. Even Coach Snider, who coached with Kevin and was there in Hershey with him, offered for a member of the cross-country team to come each day and watch the children so I could run. I told him I appreciated the offer, but even in my grief-stricken state, I knew I had to survive on my own. I had to figure out a way to survive on my own since as much as everyone meant well, I knew they would eventually go back to their own lives.

I knew that surviving it on my own also meant getting help/ therapy to eventually get mentally healthy again. That I did. I went to therapy daily. I had several different therapists, including an emotional coach. They each helped in different ways. It became a job. A job I dreaded at times but one that was necessary for my survival and our children's. It was a lot of work, but I knew I had to do it to comprehend what had happened and to get mentally (along with physically) healthy in order to help my children survive. I didn't want it to define the rest of our lives. I didn't grow up with dysfunction, and I couldn't do that to our children. There were moments when I wanted to end it all in order to end the pain, but I couldn't do that to our children or Kevin. Nobody would love them as much as I would, and Kevin would have been disappointed with me. He believed I was a strong person. Strong in running 26.2 miles, yes, but strong in surviving the unthinkable. I wasn't so sure if I would make it. Strong would be an understatement. This required more than being strong to survive.

I wanted to be able to grieve while surviving the pain. I didn't want to not grieve and have it come back years from now to haunt me. I needed to face it head on and deal with whatever it brought me and hope that my therapy would help me through it.

Kevin died right before the holidays. For some reason, I had finished Christmas shopping early that year. So, when others wanted to give the children gifts, I asked them to donate to charity instead, except for the ones from the cross-country team because I knew it would help with their healing too. Kevin was a beloved coach and was deeply missed. They were grieving as a team.

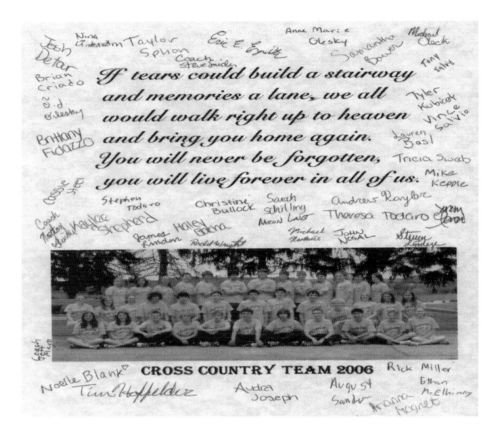

A gift from the Greensburg Salem Cross Country Team,
which Kevin helped coach the year he died.

I basically went through the motions on Thanksgiving (Kevin's favorite holiday) and then getting ready for Christmas. I did spend the holidays with Kevin's family, which was extremely hard. Despite my hope that we could grieve together, they were grieving in their own way. Going to his parents' home was sad knowing that as I entered their home, Kevin would not be there with the children and me. Their loss of a son and my loss of a husband hurt so badly that even the holidays couldn't make us feel happy. They only made us feel worse. On top of the holidays, I had so many other horrible things I had to endure because Kevin died.

I will never forget for the first time being called a widow. I was no longer married. I was now a widow. I went to the social security office to sign up for death benefits for the children and me since Kevin died young. I had to check "widow" as my new status. That moment was as horrible as the word sounds. I didn't want to be a widow. I still wanted to be married to Kevin. Being referred to as that word and now being that word was like a cruel slap in the face, letting me know yes, this was my new reality. His dying took my identity with him. I was no longer a married woman or wife. I didn't belong to the married crowd anymore or the single crowd either. It was hard to find where I fit in since most widows were older and most of my friends were married.

Another bad experience was going to widow groups. As I said, most were a lot older. I didn't feel like I belonged there. Kevin and I were just beginning our lives together. We had so much left to do together. They pretty much had a lifetime with their husbands, and their children had their dad for all of their childhood and then some. I couldn't relate. I am not lessening their pain, but as you get older, you and your partner talk about death; you assume it will happen eventually, not when you are forty and forty-six.

One of the most terrible things I had to do along with planning Christmas was pick out a headstone. A headstone—the idea of it made me nauseous. Debbie, Samantha's mom, fortunately agreed to take me. I would not have survived that experience without her. The idea of Kevin's name being etched in stone along with his date of birth and death made it seem permanent.

In my grief-stricken state, there were actually times I would try to bargain with God. *If you let Kevin come back, I will do this.* A part of me was convinced I could get God to change his plan for Kevin if I begged enough. Seeing it etched in stone made me realize I was delusional about Kevin coming back. I used to think, *Oh, if only God takes him for five years and lets him come back, I can survive this.* Survive if I knew Kevin would come back to us. Yes, it almost sounds crazy, but grief does that to you. In my most crazy moments, I thought if I had Kevin cremated, I probably would have driven around with his urn and ashes strapped in.

I also thought if I made it through Christmas, then things would return to normal—as normal as possible for the children and me. We would then be okay. Every year, Kevin and I would take the children to cut down a Christmas tree. I wanted to continue the tradition for the children. So, I took Kevin's truck, which was brought to our house a week after Kevin died. He had left it parked at the school while he drove the school van to Hershey. When it first arrived, I let my mind believe it was Kevin coming home. But it was empty inside, just like how I felt.

I got the children out of the truck and hoped I could cut a tree down for us. It ended up being a terrible experience. I couldn't cut the tree down. I'm not exactly sure what I was thinking. Looking back, I was physically there in that moment, but not mentally, so I really wasn't thinking. I was acting without thought. I was still in shock at that time from Kevin's dying so suddenly. I found myself crying and kicking at the tree, hoping it would fall over. There was no singing of Christmas songs, no joy. The children picked up on my anxiety, especially Sydney, who was six. She and Quintin, who was three, started fighting.

Eventually, after a long period of time, somehow the tree came down, and I dragged it to the truck and somehow lifted it up into the truck bed. In the meantime, matters just got worse. Sydney (who was hurting the most and understood about her daddy being gone) showed her anger and frustrations about her dad by throwing a rock at one of the truck windows and breaking it. Just like her broken little heart. I got the glass out and drove home with a broken window in freezing weather. I wasn't mad, just sad because I knew she was hurting and missing her daddy.

Once home, I couldn't even get the tree to stand up straight. Being so out of it, I took a string and tied the tree to a doorknob and other things in order to hold it up straight. Looking back, I can laugh, but at the time, it wasn't funny, just sad. I was barely holding myself up. My friend Paul came over and fixed the tree while I went on a run. How I needed to run, to find some sort of peace in my heart. He saw how desperately I needed to run and was kind enough to not only fix the tree but also watch the children.

In the beginning, there were days I couldn't run fast enough or hard enough in the hopes of escaping this new life. Running was the only place I could escape completely and not let my mind go there. I eventually found my own means to run each day. Initially, I would have David, our neighbor, come over at 5:15 a.m. before school. He would watch the children while I ran. If he couldn't come, then I would take the children to a park where Quinn and Syd would play in the middle as I ran around them with Lilly in a baby jogger. As they all got older, I took them to a park that had a half-mile loop around it. They could play while Mommy took time out for herself. I had a neighborhood route I could run that was never far from the house when they wanted to stay home. Other times, my family, Kevin's, Debbie, or others would offer to watch them so I could run. I did whatever it took at times to get a run in. I knew it would help me to get through the day better and be a better mom by taking the time to run. For running was the only place that allowed me peace from the heartache.

I kept telling myself to just get through the holidays and when the children went back to school, Sydney kindergarten and Quinn preschool, and we had a routine, life would be more normal. What exactly would normal be? I was playing mind games with myself. It has never been the normal I had when Kevin was here. As our old normal lives fell apart, so did the house. I couldn't keep up, and I didn't care or have the energy to deal with it. Our family dinners became which drive-through the kids agreed upon, and our bedtime routine consisted of all of us hugging each other in my bed until we fell asleep and escaped the sadness. Over time, I came to grips with the new normal and was able to get the house back in order. The house being in order helped me function better in our new life. I realized my environment was the only thing I had control over. Having control of my environment made me feel better in my new life. For I learned on November 3, 2006, that most things are out of my control. In time, family dinners no longer consisted of us frequenting drive-throughs but actually sitting down as a family, and we all eventually fell asleep in our own beds. With time and therapy, we all became accustomed to our new normal.

School, however, actually made things worse for me. Kevin was the epitome of school. He not only coached cross country and track for the high school, but he also taught at the elementary school where Sydney went. So, despite the normal routine school offered, life would never be the normal I knew with Kevin. Like all my therapists told me, "There is now a new normal." To be honest, I hated everything the new normal meant.

Something as simple as the bus stop caused me to think of Kevin and become completely depressed. Sydney was in kindergarten where Kevin had taught. Fortunately, Jessica (one of Kevin's coworkers and close friends) would pick Sydney up each day so I wouldn't have to deal with the bus stop. I got Sydney up in enough time to get dressed and get her out the door. I hated it. It broke my heart that she would go to the school where her dad taught and he would no longer be there. She would get a daily reminder of her daddy being gone, gone forever. It made me beyond sad. He would often drive her to school with him so he could spend more time with her. That would no longer be.

There would be moments throughout that first year that I had to muster up enough courage to go to the school where my husband and the father of my children no longer taught. I dreaded all the days I went to the school. My heart just hurt walking in that school.

The most difficult thing I endured was getting Kevin's belongings back. The bag he took with him to the race, the clothes he had worn that very day to run, and the running shoes he'd had on at the time. It was gut-wrenching and made me weak and sad all over. Kevin, the cute runner who noticed me and whom I fell in love with, would never wear these clothes again, and I would never see that handsome runner coming toward me again. My heart dropped, just like when Harry said Kevin wasn't going to call, just like that, but this time I knew Kevin and had had a life with him. I felt nothing but lost. Life would never be the same.

20
The Children

As for Sydney, she was six, and you would have thought she was a little adult in the way she handled the whole situation. She dealt with her dad dying way better than I did. She loved her daddy and missed him terribly but was more matter-of-fact about it than I was. Just like her daddy would have been. "It is what it is, and there's no changing it, so keep moving forward," Kevin would have said. Looking back, I think she was just trying to be strong for me. She was always my easy child. Sydney has turned out remarkably, and her daddy would be so proud of the young lady she has become. Not to say she hasn't had her share of moments of being sad. Not so long ago, she and I had a conversation, and I told her that I never asked her to be strong for me and that I was sorry if she felt like she had to be. I did depend on her at times to help me with the other two, and the other two required more attention being younger, but I never wanted her not to grieve her daddy. I told her I wanted her to cry and to show more emotion, for at times, she could be cold, and that wasn't healthy.

That was a break-through conversation because she told me others constantly told her to be good for her mommy. They probably meant it in a good way, but she was a little girl who had just lost her daddy. She needed to act out her emotions. In that moment, she started to cry to me and said that she knew I never asked that of her. She is a strong young lady, and sometimes I worry too strong, so it was good for her to let the walls down and let me in. She needed to cry and grieve like a little girl. I also feel guilt the most with her because I quit being the mommy she knew before her dad died. I didn't have the energy to read to her or play with her like I used to. She never complained and tells me she understands it wasn't my fault that grief overtook her mommy. I have cried to her about missing out with her and that I can't get those moments back. I didn't mean to miss out. I just couldn't help it. Like she said, grief overtook my whole being. I was present physically but not always mentally. I just want to hug that little girl more. She gets that.

She does remember her daddy the most; they had an incredibly close bond. She went to therapy for a while, but then she seemed okay with the new normal. Not to say she didn't miss her dad—she just accepted God's plan better than I did. She did ask her Uncle Richard, "If a heart is broken, can it get fixed?" He told her it was just a feeling—that it really isn't broken. She replied her heart broke when her daddy died, but her mommy's really broke.

Sydney has also made it a habit to do the sign of the cross and say a prayer when she sees an ambulance with sirens on. She does this because she hopes someone did it for her daddy as he was being rushed to the hospital. There have been moments over the years where it has really hit her hard. When she had another dad coaching her, she wanted her daddy to be there too. At one of her first track meets, she told me she felt sick, but I went on to find out she didn't want to run because it reminded her of her daddy.

Another moment that broke both our hearts came with her running. Since our children were very little, even before Kevin died, everyone wanted our kids to run. Our children were soccer kids, and just because we ran didn't mean they needed to relive our dream. While in seventh grade, Sydney decided to go out for track, and in that first year of running, she broke the school record and went on to win the county meet overall in the mile in a time of five minutes and thirty-nine seconds. As she was coming to the finish line, I could feel the pain in her legs, knew the joy she felt in her heart, and saw victory on her face. I smiled with pride at our daughter's success and cried inside and out knowing the joy Kevin would have shown on his face in that moment. He would have smiled ear to ear and been so happy for her and her success. If only he could have been there to share in that special moment. How I needed and wanted him to be there to share with his little girl in her happiness.

Despite her being so happy, I could tell she was wishing her dad was there as well. I told her that her daddy was smiling down on her. In that moment, maybe we were handing the torch off to her, but only if she wanted it. That burning torch for running never died with Kevin, and maybe over time it will go on to burn bright in Sydney if she desires it badly enough.

When I have doubts about being a good enough mom to Sydney, she does something to eliminate those doubts. On one of my birthdays, she gave me this card:

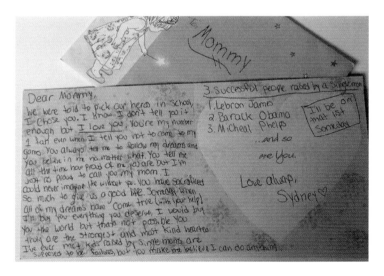

Quintin was three when his daddy died. I don't think in that moment he quite comprehended what had happened with his daddy. Why didn't Daddy ever come home? He was too young to completely understand. He has gone to the most therapy and has dealt with his dad's death the worst, maybe because he was so confused—or maybe he's just a little boy who so desperately needs his daddy. He now seems to be in a better place and no longer seems to need therapy.

Quintin and Sydney went to see Lori Iezzi. She was an extremely nice lady and always put together. I would show up all disheveled, and on one occasion, in the dead of winter, Quintin showed up with no shoes. Obviously, I was anything but put together. She would play games to help them with their grieving.

Quintin has been in and out of therapy over the years. He seems fine, and then something triggers him to go backward. One time in third grade, a fellow classmate said to Quintin, "Well, at least my dad didn't die." Quintin became hysterical. Mr. Thomas, the principal, called me, and I rushed to the school. That incident made Quintin go way back in the grieving process. Mr. Thomas and I agreed to have him seek additional therapy. The therapy would occur during school. This way, Quintin would have to attend and not be able to fight me on it, for there were times when we were on our way to therapy when he would threaten to jump out of the car at a stop sign. It became too stressful. This way was best for all of us.

I tried several types of therapy for them just like I did for myself. I even took them to art therapy, but like with me, some were better than others. Lori helped them the most. Quintin also fed a lot off of my anxiety, so the calmer I was and the better place I was in, so was he.

Despite him doing better, he will still probably have moments of sadness. It helps that he has some really good male role models in his coaches, uncles, and teachers. These men seem to really care about him and look out for him. Like I said, Quintin didn't fully grasp why his daddy never came home. Heck, I was almost forty years old and didn't quite comprehend it all either. He left and never came back. Quintin had major separation anxiety because of his confusion. Getting him to go to preschool was a constant struggle. He was so worried I would never come back. He would cling to me and hold on to me as if he were never going to let go of me in fear I wouldn't come home like his daddy. Initially, when I would go run, I would have to show him on a watch when Mommy would be back, where the big hand and little hand would be. That seemed to make him feel better. He sometimes wondered and worried when his mom was coming back if we're at an amusement park or store.

I am not sure if Quintin remembers his daddy like Sydney does since he was only three. He sometimes cries and says he doesn't remember him, and I tell him to look in the mirror. He looks just like his dad, and everything about him is his daddy. I especially think of Kevin when Quintin is running and his hair flies in the air like his dad's or when he's standing with his hands in his pockets just like his dad did. It is a blessing; he reminds us so much of Kevin.

Quintin, eight years old, at Kevin's memorial kids' race, looking just like his dad.

Lillian was only twenty-one months when her daddy died. She was too young to even understand what happened. She has never gone to therapy. Lilly found therapy in water. She constantly wanted to be bathed. She loved playing in the water. Michele (a medium I would later go see) told me that Lilly saw her daddy in the water. At times, it was overwhelming. She would just finish being bathed by myself or my friend Flo then no sooner want back in the tub. Perhaps that is why to this day, Lilly loves playing in the water. Maybe she still sees her daddy in it. She says she remembers her dad, but sometimes I wonder if it's because of all the stories we tell about him. I tell her how she used to crawl all over her daddy and he would play with her. Once she entered kindergarten and saw other kids with both mommies and daddies, she started to struggle and miss her daddy. She has cried to me at times wanting him back, but for the most part, Lilly has been fine.

Lilly, my gift from God (about eighteen months old).

There will continue to be moments throughout their lives when they will miss their dad and need him. However, their father's death will not destroy their lives, just alter them and change who they are in a way. They have dealt with loss at very young ages, so they realize that things happen that are out of our control. That life doesn't always work out the way you think it will and there will be disappointments and heartache along the way. That the glass can be half empty.

The only blessing with them being so young when Kevin died is that they don't really know what it's like to have a dad. Kind of like an only child doesn't know what they are missing out on by not having a sibling. I feel like it's a blessing and a curse. It's a blessing that they were so young, but sad that they don't remember much. It saddens me because Kevin was an exceptional and loving dad. Their lives would have been impacted greatly if he were alive. I know what they are missing, since I grew up with an amazing and loving dad.

They do all know that their daddy held them and loved them and didn't choose to leave them. It was not his plan but God's. I tell them that he is always watching over them and is present in their hearts. So yes, there will always be something missing, but for the most part, if you met them, you would never know their dad died. They are normal, happy children. They are children who are not only deeply loved by me, but also by Kevin's family, who continue to play an important role in their lives by attending their sporting events, taking them places for a day of fun, shopping with them, and spending time with them on holidays. They continue to keep Kevin's presence in the children's lives by their presence. Initially, they grieved on their own, struggling with their own loss. Over time, we were able to come together and make the welfare of the children our common goal. Over the last twelve years, we have celebrated the holidays and special occasions in the children's lives, sat together at many of their activities, and stayed family despite our grief.

When Kevin first died, the days seemed forever and couldn't be over quickly enough. Now where has the time gone? Our children have grown up so quickly. I sometimes wish I could go back to when they were little, but I could not relive November 3, 2006, again.

I remember immediately having all kinds of thoughts when Kevin died. Who would walk my daughters down the aisle or teach Quintin how to be a gentleman? Through all my therapy, I have learned not to go there and to cross that bridge when it comes.

Christmas 2005 - Sydney (five), Lillian (ten months), and Quintin (over two and a half).

Christmas 2015 – Lillian (ten), Sydney (fifteen), and Quintin (twelve).

21
More Heartache

February 19, 2007, was the day my already shattered heart completely crumbled. My dad's death would have destroyed me in itself, but by that time, I was already completely devastated and out of it due to Kevin's death three months earlier.

My dad's back had been hurting him at Kevin's viewing. We all thought it was from a fall he'd had the summer before. Little did we know, just like Kevin, he was slowly dying inside, but this time, cancer was the culprit. My family held off telling me for a month. They were afraid of how fragile I already was. I was broken, and now the idea of losing my dad was more than I could handle. I broke down crying, "No, not now my dad. My other rock. No!" How could this have happened? How? The two most important men in my life, one was gone and realistically, soon the other would be as well. How? Just a few short months ago, life was good and I had them both in my life.

The only difference between Kevin's and my dad's dying was that I could process it. I saw the physical changes and the toll cancer was taking on my dad and realized he needed to die.

I will never forget my dad lying in bed crying, holding my hand, saying, "You and Kevin were robbed. I will fight this so I can help you raise your children and take them fishing this summer." He wanted to take them fishing at Lake Edinboro. Growing up, each summer we would go there because my Grandma Collins had a cottage there. Some of my best childhood memories were created there. We would go swimming, play miniature golf, build sandcastles, go to the local dairy farm with Dad to get chocolate milk, and walk to the penny candy store. We also always went fishing with Daddy. We loved fishing with our dad. It was so much fun. He taught us how to bait our lines, and we always released the fish back into the water.

Another time when my dad was in bed home from the hospital, he said to all of us (all five children and my mom), "The success of a man is to have a wife who has loved him for forty-two years and five children who love one another and who love their parents." That we did. We all loved him so much. As he said this, tears rolled down his cheeks. I think at this moment; he knew it would be a short time before he would die.

When he took a turn for the worse, he was hospitalized. I remember spending all night in the hospital holding his hand, telling him how much I loved him, how lucky I was to have him as a dad while reading to him from the Bible. I got to say goodbye and tell him everything I wanted to, unlike with Kevin. Never saying goodbye is heartbreaking. As hard as it was to see the man I called "Dad" deteriorate, it helped with the accepting of his death. Eventually, we all knew we needed to let him go and let him die with dignity, as the doctor said. One of the saddest moments was seeing my brother, Jeff, cry. He was going to lose his best friend. My dad was his best man in his wedding. They did everything together. That really tore at me.

As the doctor suggested we let him die with dignity, we decided to allow him to let go of this world in order to move on to the next. We decided to quit trying everything to keep him alive. Just like with Kevin, I would have taken my dad alive here in any form, but I knew deep down inside that was me being selfish, but it wasn't best for Kevin and definitely not for my dad. He was exhausted.

He came home that day on hospice. We were all around the bed waiting for his mom, my grandma, to come and say goodbye. The moment my grandma said goodbye and left the room, my dad passed. He was holding on for her. Before he passed, I asked him to tell Kevin how much I love him and miss him. He squeezed my hand to let me know he would. My dad, in all my life, never let me down, and I knew he would relay the message to Kevin no matter what it took. I will forever treasure getting to say goodbye to my dad. When you don't get to say goodbye, you realize how blessed you are when you do have the opportunity to have closure. I would have given anything to have held Kevin's hand and told him I loved him, but I don't know if Kevin could have handled knowing he was leaving us or if I could have handled seeing Kevin get sick. I am sure God knew that.

I could hardly process all of this. Approximately three months ago, life was good and I had the two most important men in my life there with me. Now they were gone *forever.*

The funeral was depressing, and walking down the aisle holding hands with my mom behind the casket was heart-wrenching. We now had a common bond. "'Til death do us part" had come too soon once again. My dad was only sixty-nine, and my mom was sixty-three. She would never get to celebrate their fiftieth wedding anniversary or grow old with my dad. It was sad seeing my mom now a widow too. (How I *hate* that word.)

The only blessing in all of this was that Kevin, not my dad, died first. With the suddenness of Kevin's dying, I was kind of out of it, in a state of shock still. If my dad had died prior to Kevin, I truly think both of their dying would have completely destroyed me, for I would have been more present and not so out of it. I, too, probably would have died. I now understand why older couples often die within a short time of each other. I believe I would have died after Kevin if it weren't for three little lives (our children) needing me more than ever. Plus, thank God they died close to each other and not a year or so apart. I would have been more mentally present, making it that much more devastating. I saw my own devastation on my mom's face. Her pretty, bright-blue eyes were now cloudy with tears, and her perfect smile was absent. She looked sad and heartbroken like me.

So, in a three-month span, I lost the two men I loved the most, my two rocks and my biggest fans. I believe if my dad had lived and we could have gone fishing that summer and done so many other things together, our children would have greatly benefited by his presence in their lives.

A little while after my dad died, my mom gave me a note I had written years ago to him telling him how much I loved him and that he was the best dad anyone could have. It made me cry to think he held on to that for all these years. I was so glad he knew exactly how much he meant to me.

I never knew my dad not to have gray hair. His gray hair and gregarious personality made him loved by many. He loved his family and was always there for each of us. He made each of us feel as if we were his favorite. He loved the song "The Candy Man" by Sammy Davis Jr. and would sing it to all five of us. Just like the candy man, he mixed everything with love and made the world a sweeter place.

One of the last things my dad said was, "All I wanted to do was have some kids and some laughs." That he did.

With my dad, John Collins.

With my mom, Susanne Collins. I was eight months pregnant with Sydney.

My dad, John, and my mom, Susanne Collins - June 1996.

22
How I Survived It All

The double whammy of my husband along with my dad dying took a major toll on me. I would wake up all sweaty from anxiety and stress. I was so afraid of what might happen next. My family and Joe were concerned about how much weight I was losing. I was tiny to begin with and couldn't afford to lose weight and risk getting sick. So, three months after my dad died and six months after Kevin died, my brother-in-law Joe, who is a doctor, suggested I get on an anti-anxiety pill to take the edge off, cope better, and not be so anxious.

I didn't want to get on an antidepressant because I wanted to be able to grieve now, not ten years from now. After talking with my doctor, I went on Lexapro. I knew it was something I needed temporarily to help me survive. The more anxious I was, the more anxious Quintin became. He fed off my anxiety. Lexapro took the edge off. I never looked at it as a crutch, but something I needed to help me deal with my new reality without Kevin or my dad.

I ended up being on it for a year, and then I decided I no longer needed it and went off it cold turkey, ironically, on Father's Day. My doctor wasn't thrilled because you are supposed to wean yourself off of it. I don't recommend going off an anti-anxiety cold turkey for others. When I made the decision to go off Lexapro, I mentally decided there was no going back to how I felt prior to the medicine.

I was determined not to rely on the medicine anymore. I never suffered withdrawal from the medicine and never allowed the anxiety to creep back in and take over my life. Maybe I was mentally in a better place, stronger, and able to handle any fears or doubts I had regarding the future, or maybe it was because my daily love for running came back. My running helped stomp away any fears or anxiety that started creeping back in. Running was huge in my finding peace again.

I definitely benefited from taking Lexapro because I no longer worried about what might happen next. The children benefited too. The calmer I was, the better they were, especially Quintin. I was still able to grieve Kevin's and my dad's deaths. I knew this was necessary despite how difficult it would be. Facing the grief head-on would help with my healing process. Grief is overwhelming, and there is no normal way to grieve. Everyone's grief is different depending on the relationship shared with the one lost. There is no book on how to grieve, and nobody has to understand the way you do it except yourself.

I knew I had to do a lot of work and seek a lot of help to get in a better place. I reached out to several therapists for help. They all helped me in their own unique way. I was going to a different type of therapy each day. At times, that wasn't enough. Daily therapy was necessary for me to survive Kevin's and my dad's deaths. I needed to survive the horrible heartache and pain so I could help our children survive. I would wake up afraid of what would lie ahead. I was scared. I was a single parent with three children. Nothing made me smile or happy. I just wanted each day to be over with. Time couldn't go fast enough (now, looking back, I wonder where have the last twelve years gone?). In that moment, time went so slowly. I would often run to Pink's song "Who Knew," and when she sang the line, "If someone said three years from now, you'd be long gone," I couldn't wait to get to three years out.

Everyone told me time helps. Initially, that bothered me, but I found out time really does heal if you do the grief work. I remember being told by my therapist to take one minute at a time and eventually to live one day at a time. The first year, that advice helped with each special occasion: our anniversary, Kevin's birthday, school starting, and, of course, the holidays. That first year and probably even more so the second (since I was more mentally present) were the worst years of my life. I let every important date control me as far as emotions go. I dreaded the day before it even arrived, whether it was Kevin's birthday or some other significant date.

In the beginning, we would do something to recognize the children's dad's birthday, such as letting balloons go to him or getting a little cake or ice cream on Father's Day. We don't do that anymore. It's just a date, and it is no different than any other day. We miss Kevin the same, regardless of the day. I still tend to live one day at a time in order to not get overwhelmed with all that comes with being a single parent.

Things that used to make me happy, like the chirping of birds or Christmas music, now made me sad. I *hated* it all. Even the joy of being a mom was taken away briefly. I love my children, but I hated the idea of no longer having their dad as a partner to share in their moments. I never wanted to be a single parent.

I also found that I could only talk to certain people and let them see me grieve. That inner circle of people made me feel safe and that eventually things would be okay. Some, if not most of that inner circle, was my family, some dear friends, but mostly my therapists. They didn't judge that I had moments of wanting to end it all. (That's how bad the pain was.) They didn't judge that I hated God for taking my young husband and the father of my children. They didn't judge that I hated life. They didn't judge at all. They listened to my story over and over, and each one provided me with a means to survive this horrible journey I was on.

I had an emotional coach whom I spoke to weekly. She had lost her husband too, so she understood what I was going through.

I had another therapist who had me write a goodbye letter to Kevin. In the letter, I told him everything I would have if given the chance. It provided closure since I never did get to say goodbye, which is one of the hardest things I will ever have to live with. The same therapist eventually helped me overcome the fear of going back to the place I was when I got that horrible phone call. With her help, I was able to return to the place where a phone call changed my life forever. Other therapists helped me deal with the idea of returning to places with the children that Kevin and I went to. It took a while, but over time, I could return to those spots.

It became a part of my daily routine to see a therapist and talk about what had happened. I told my story over and over while searching for answers (I realized I will never get some answers until I see Kevin again) and searched for ways to cope and to help our children cope with our new family dynamic.

There's a grief counseling program in Pittsburgh that I had heard wonderful things about, so the children and I went there. It ended up being one of the worst experiences of my life. I couldn't get the children and me out of there soon enough. I thought they would put the children and me with other young families who had either lost their mom or dad. Instead it was a mix of people who had lost their ninety-year-old grandma or grandfather or even some who lost pets. I am not implying that those losses aren't sad or taking away from their pain, but I couldn't relate. It just wasn't the same. I lost my young husband, the father of my children, my best friend, my future, and so many other dreams we had. I hated it. I am not saying that others haven't had a good experience at that program. It just wasn't for my children or me. After that, I learned to watch the type of help I sought for us because this avenue of help actually made us all feel worse.

Some were definitely more helpful than others, and I ended up seeing those more often, but each did contribute to my/our surviving. For that, I will be forever grateful. It was a journey I couldn't do alone. There were days when the children and I moved forward and days when we went backward in the healing process. The therapy my children and I sought allowed us to go backward (part of the grieving process) while continuing to move forward and not get stuck there in that dark place. They taught me to be patient with myself and grieve the way that was best for me/us.

My therapist gave me hope life would get better. I remember Dr. Reiss saying to me, "It will get better than it is right now—just not as quickly as you would like or as we would wish for you . . . but it will not stay like this forever."

Another person who helped tremendously was Monsignor Statnick. He helped me deal with my anger at God. He said it was normal to feel that way and God was okay with it. God understood it was part of my grieving. I didn't understand—why Kevin? Which I know sounds selfish. Why anybody? But through talking with Monsignor, I learned to accept that sometimes things are out of our hands and are in God's hands. There are so many unanswered questions that I have learned to quit asking over the years.

Often when I waited for Sydney to get off the bus from half-day kindergarten, I would hear the church bells chiming in the distance. Normally, the sound of the bells brought me peace, but at that time, they brought only sadness. As time went on, my anger toward God faded and the sound of the bells brought me hope because I knew God was still there and had never left me despite my anger.

Samantha, the young girl who was running with Kevin that day, also helped. We actually helped each other. We would go on runs and talk about that day as much as she could and about our grief and emotions. I knew she needed it, and I did too. I was extremely concerned and worried about Samantha, who had witnessed such a horrific moment, and on top of it, to be so young. I wanted to make sure she would be okay and not be traumatized by that day. It was a bond that grew stronger between her and me because we both understood the other's pain. We had shared a devastating loss. She had lost the coach she adored, and I had lost the husband I loved and the dad who was amazing to our children.

To this day, Samantha and I remain close. We share a bond that became stronger due to a tragic event. Samantha is in a great place now and has been able to move on and live a normal life while realizing at a young age how fragile life is. Neither she nor I will ever forget that difficult time. There are still moments when we both feel safe talking to the other about it and sharing our emotions while still being able to move forward and not get stuck back in those dark days. Kevin would be so proud of the wonderful young lady she has become.

Uncle Richard also helped with all of our surviving. He was a lifelong friend of Kevin's who instantly became my friend. I would wake up afraid and immediately call him. He would come over in the evenings and help with the children, and his presence helped me to not be so afraid. The evening was the hardest part of the day for me to get through since that was when Kevin would usually be home and our family was complete. He made the dark days a little brighter by bringing joy and laughter back into the house. He would play games with the children, listen to my cries of sadness, and offer words of hope that life would get better in time. He made the house seem not so empty. I am not sure if I would have been able to get through those dark days without him taking time away from his life to help us all survive ours. We are so lucky to have him. He is forever a part of our family.

Debbie, Samantha's mom, also went out of her way to help. I think it was therapeutic for her, too. She was not only concerned about us but about her daughter, and helping her daughter's coach's family out meant a lot to Samantha. Debbie would often watch the kids so I could run. She understood I needed to *run*. I needed to escape, even if only for an hour. She also helped me with errands when the idea of going to the grocery store seemed impossible. I was normally a high-energy person; grief zapped the life out of me and left me exhausted and depressed. On the days I didn't want to run, she made me run, knowing it was the best medicine for me. In the beginning, I just wanted to run away, but as the grief took over, I didn't want to run because running took Kevin away, and with his being taken away, the runner in me went away briefly too. Like with Samantha, I still remain close to Debbie and will be forever grateful for her caring.

My dear friend Kathy (my sorority sister and lifelong friend) was always available to lend an ear, hug, or pep talk when needed. She helped me to live one minute and then eventually one day at a time. She taught me to breathe so I wouldn't become overwhelmed in my new life. She and her friendship have been a gift to me, and not only has she helped me through this trying time in my life, but she and her friendship had also been there before to help me through difficult times. I treasure her.

My family all tried to help as much as they could by simply loving us and making sure we were fine by either inviting us to spend time with their families or by taking the children to give me a break and to allow me to run. I am blessed with the best family.

My twin sister, Suzanne, is the one who found my emotional coach, Mie, and she also helped me befriend a young widow from her area in California. Monica's husband, Matt, died unexpectedly in a car accident two weeks prior to Kevin's dying. I often think that for two weeks as her life was falling apart, I was happy, loving life, and had my husband. Suzanne had read about her story, and after Kevin died, she got her contact information so we could talk. Two young widows with young children whose husbands had died unexpectedly, and now we were alone to raise their children. We both were living the same nightmare. We completely understood what the other was going through: life without a husband or father to our children. Both of our lives had forever changed unexpectedly in an instant.

Monica and I have become friends and have formed a lifetime bond because of our common tragic circumstances. She has been a blessing in my survival. The bond we share will never be broken. She was the one person I knew who truly got it. Whether it was anger, heartbreak, fear, loneliness, or sadness, she understood, for she was feeling those same things. When either one of us felt alone, we knew we truly weren't alone because we had each other. Knowing her has been a gift. Her importance in my life is *huge*. Two women on two different coasts whose lives went from being wonderful to anything but and, because of that common pain and tragedy, two women who might have never met because of the distance became close friends for life.

I am very happy to say twelve years later, Monica and her girls are remarkably well, and she has found love again. I couldn't wish this happiness on anyone as much as her. What she and I have gone through is something I would never wish on anyone. It is a living hell.

Then there is Joe, my coach, my family, my dear friend, my sounding board, and another important man in my life. He has remained a constant in my life, and I am thankful for that. He and his family immediately came to my side the moment I called and told them the news. He has never wavered in being there for me in times of need. I know I can count on him for anything. Just like on that first day at the CMU track, he believed in my ability to qualify more than I did in that moment, and now he believed in me being strong enough to survive this.

Again, I had my doubts, but sometimes you have no choice but to be strong. (I had three other lives counting on me.) Yes, I knew I was physically strong and mentally tough. In order to compete as a marathoner, I had to be, but this was different. This was my life, not a race, but as Alberto Salazar, the one-time world's best marathoner, said, "Life is the only long run that matters." So, maybe being a marathoner would help me survive. As a marathoner, I had to put in a lot of miles and hard work, never knowing how much it would translate to life in general. Instead of miles, it was a lot of therapy, and just like in the marathon, there were moments where I felt like I hit a wall and could not go one step further, but surviving this was 90 percent mental, just like running. I could choose to survive this and finish this race of life no matter what came my way, or I could quit and never finish. I chose to survive and finish the race, for I had never quit before, so why start now in this most important race, my life?

Joe helped me along in this race by convincing me that I needed something positive to focus on (a distraction), a goal to have, and that was to start racing again. The one constant, the one positive thing in my life that never completely went away with Kevin and my dad's dying, was running. Why not get back into competitive running? It had been good for me before, and it would be good for me now, a positive, something I could control, my comfort zone, my place to escape, and the one part of me that hadn't died with the two men whom I loved most.

Running was the best therapy I could take on. It made me feel fully alive again, despite my feeling like I had died, too. Starting to train for races with Sev's help again was the best distraction for me. A fire inside of me slowly started to come alive all because of Joe's and Sev's believing in me once more. Also, it was good for the children to see me doing something for myself. Running is the only thing I do for myself. Because I do take the time to run, it helps me be a better mom. Their seeing me commit to training and coming to cheer me on at the different races also has been a positive for them. Over the last twelve years or so, I have done the Pittsburgh Marathon (won the masters each time in two hours, fifty-seven minutes, and seven seconds – sixth place overall; two hours, fifty-six minutes, and forty-eight seconds – fourth overall; two hours, fifty-seven minutes, and forty-eight seconds – tenth overall), the Pittsburgh Half Marathon a couple of times, Marine Corps Marathon (in 2014, I placed ninth overall and broke three hours, two weeks shy of turning forty-eight), and other local and out-of-town races, all with my children cheering me on and, I am positive, Kevin and my dad too.

Sydney and Lillian congratulate me after the 2009 Pittsburgh Marathon.

2016 Aspire Harrisburg Marathon – second woman overall, age fifty.

The most symbolic of the races I did was Kevin's memorial race. This race was started by Coach Snider and Jeremy Lenzi, both of whom coached with Kevin. The first one was held on Memorial Day 2007 and the last one on Memorial Day 2011. It was a perfect way to remember Kevin by having a 5K in his honor. It also was a great way for those who cared about Kevin, whether as a coach, teacher, friend, coworker, etc., to come together and remember him. It was a beautiful gesture. I can vividly recall during the first race my turning the bend toward the finish and seeing Jeremy, Coach Snider, our children, my family, Kevin's family, and so many others smiling and cheering, loudly rejoicing in my win. I had a smile on my face as tears rolled down my checks. Yes, I was glad to win, but I never imagined I would compete in a race honoring my deceased husband. Their rejoicing reconfirmed to me in that moment that I would survive this. By winning that race each time, I felt I was showing Kevin that I was okay and that I was winning this new race of life. After five years, Kevin's family and I wanted it to end on a high note, and that it did.

There is a part of me that is forever changed, but the one thing that has helped me get back to who I was has been running. Running is a huge part of who I am. It makes me feel alive and whole, despite having had a part of me die along with Kevin and my dad. I feel that my two biggest fans are so happy that I got back into competitive running and that they are thrilled that not only did I go on to get inducted into my high school hall of fame (Plum High), but also into the Pittsburgh Marathon Hall of Fame along with the East Boro's Chapter of the Pennnsylvania Hall of Fame. I know they are proud of my running achievements, but even more so proud of my surviving the unthinkable. They are still my biggest fans in running and in life.

23
The Other Side

Now that Kevin and my dad had died, I wondered, what exactly was Heaven like? I read about it in the Bible and knew it was supposedly beautiful and those that had gone and returned said there was this feeling of euphoria. I never thought about it much, but now I needed answers. So, I went to see a medium, Michele Dugan of Greensburg, Pennsylvania. I know being Catholic, we're not supposed to believe in this, but I needed answers, closure, and I needed to say goodbye to Kevin.

I went to see Michele because another widow I had befriended had gone to her and I so desperately needed to talk to Kevin, even if just to say goodbye. There was no crystal ball and turban—just a warm, approachable woman. She was down to earth and very comforting in the way she spoke. She immediately made me a believer in her gift. She had never met me before and didn't know Kevin. The things she said she could only know by talking to one of us.

The first time I went (the first of many times to come), she told me that Kevin was sorry for leaving; it wasn't his plan but that someday I would understand the plan. She also said that when I do get to the other side, he will come and get me and say, "Hi, Little Bit." As soon as she said that, I began to cry. Kevin would always answer the door when we were dating and say that. How could a complete stranger know what he called me? How? This made me believe he was talking through her to me. The fact that he said it wasn't his plan made me feel better because even though I knew he didn't choose to leave us, I had initially been mad at him, feeling abandoned, betrayed. This wasn't our plan, and it wasn't his choice or mine. It was God's.

I became obsessed with talking to Michele after that first visit where I got to say goodbye. In my mind, it was as if she were talking with him on the phone. I even thought if I could just talk to him each day, then I could possibly survive this. It would make things easier to deal with. I became so crazy thinking that Kevin was at her house that I found myself running to her home looking for him. See, in the beginning, I kept bargaining with God to allow Kevin to come back. So, I actually thought he might, but as time went on and through Kevin talking through Michele, I realized if that were God's plan, then Kevin would come back, but that wasn't the case. My bargaining with God wouldn't let me accept that Kevin was gone and allow me to move forward. Through Michele, I learned that acceptance eventually has to come. We can't will it. It just has to come. I had to accept he was gone or I could continue to fight it, but it would be an awful way to live without acceptance or peace.

The better the children and I became, the better Kevin became and the more he could move on, too. Initially, when he passed, Michele said he was confused. He was not sure what had happened to him and immediately came to the children and me because he was concerned. He died instantly and never felt any pain. He understood once his Grandma Heiman, whom he adored, greeted him. He hung around the children and me a lot in the beginning until we were better, which allowed him to move on. He was initially stunned, confused, and kind of in both worlds, but eventually he realized he couldn't have both, so he moved on.

Kevin has come through Michele and said, "He did fight to stay alive, but it was not his choice; it was God's. Once he understood the plan, he didn't wish to be saved. You'll understand that there is nothing he can do. Keep letting him go and do not hang on so he doesn't steal your future."

At first, I was so worried about Kevin, and that was when someone came through to Michele and said, "Kevin is better than okay. It is the ultimate; let God take care of him." When I initially had those feelings of wanting to die, Kevin told Michele to tell me to quit wishing I would die. That wasn't part of the plan. Kevin would be happier when the children and I were happy. Kevin also told her to tell me, "Quit fighting with something neither one of us can fix. God knows what He is doing. Who are we to supersede?"

When my dad died, Michele said he went immediately to "happy" because he wanted to die, unlike Kevin, who had no idea he was going to die; that was why he lingered in this world. My dad was ready to move on, to leave this world, the pain, and the tiredness he felt. She also told me that Kevin helped organize the gathering, the celebration with those who had passed before my dad and knew him. My dad came through with a sense of peace. She told me that they both are around, watching over the children and me. My dad is my guardian angel. He is now looking out for me and protecting me from afar, just like he did here on earth.

They both let us know they were around by having light bulbs go out all the time in the beginning. It was bizarre how many went out.

She said they are both rooting for me and that they have said that happiness comes from within. Being happy can be a job, but it is up to me to make the choice to be happy. One of the ways of becoming happy is accepting that they both are gone and that someday I will understand why it happened. My dad also told Michele that I have the tools to be successful: courage, patience, sense of humor, and strength. I have to choose to survive this.

Michele helped me tremendously. Through her, I found closure with Kevin and peace and acceptance that it was God's plan and there was no changing it, regardless of how much I begged God. I realized that my dad and Kevin were better than fine because they had achieved the ultimate. Initially, I felt Kevin got robbed, but Michele said he was being rewarded, for he did all that he was meant to do here on earth and was now where we all strive to go. So, I shouldn't look at it as if he got cheated. He didn't. He received the highest reward for completing God's plan for him here on earth. That makes his dying so young easier to accept.

Michele is one of the reasons I have survived it all. We remain friends, and I am forever grateful for her role in my survival. I have learned not to rely on her for answers about what's to come in my life. My dependence on her became unhealthy. I never lived my life according to a medium before Kevin died. I used to listen to my heart and gut. So, I now try to live that way, listening to my inner thoughts. Michele always wanted to help me but didn't want me waiting on her every word to decide how to live my life either. She taught me a lot about what happens when one dies. I never thought of Heaven or what souls do there as much as I did when Kevin died. Because of her gift, she was able to give me the gift of acceptance and life with peace.

I told myself that somehow, I was going to be happy again. I choose happiness over anger and bitterness, but it took a lot of work and my processing all that had happened. Michele and all my therapists helped make that processing easier for me. Everyone deals differently with grief, and no one should judge how you cope with your loss. Grief is extremely messy, and there is no easy or normal way to grieve. Everyone's relationship is different, and nobody has to understand your grief. Give yourself permission to be who you are in that moment. Give yourself permission to grieve and take care of yourself. I realized if I didn't take care of myself, there was no way I could take care of three children during this grieving process. Grieving is extremely hard. It takes a lot of energy. It's all-consuming and so hard to explain because everyone does it differently. I learned it's the price you pay—the heartache and pain when you truly love someone and lose them.

I learned to not take it personally. Kevin's dying didn't happen because he or I did something wrong. It just happened. It's supposed to be this way. It's God's plan. It doesn't mean life for now will be all bad; there is still good there. Some things in life have no answers, like trying to explain the unexplainable. I need to be at peace with what is and keep moving forward. To accept what happened and that there is no changing it. That it's not a punishment, just life, and someday I will understand. I will understand why it all happened.

In the beginning, there was no acceptance, no peace with what was. Today, I have embraced acceptance in order to be able to fully live and allow our children to fully live because we have a lot to live for. It is what God wants for me, along with Kevin and my dad: to accept what is. Michele's gift allowed me to realize that.

24

Running Until I Cross the Finish Line

Running brought Kevin and me together in life, and running is what separated us, but it also has been the means to my survival. Why do we do anything in life? Simply put, because we are drawn to it and it's part of our very being. Kevin was meant to run, for it made him who he was. If you took the runner out of Kevin, you would change who he was, the person who we all loved and lost.

Running truly has been the best therapy in my surviving it all. Initially, I couldn't run fast enough from this new life, but with time, I found running to be my comfort zone, my escape, and my safe haven. When I run, nothing can affect me. I don't think about life. I just run.

One of my favorite places to run is Frick Park. It's a trail park outside of Pittsburgh. It is my greatest place to escape. My Heaven on earth where I feel no pain, just complete happiness. When I run there, I imagine Kevin running in Heaven alongside me. Just he and I running together like old times. I feel extra close to Kevin there. At first, to feel closer to Kevin, I ran with his wedding ring along with his thumbprint, which Pantalone's had made in gold, on a chain around my neck. Now, I feel close to him all the time because I know he is always with me, whether in my heart or beside me looking out for the children and me. I had a thumbprint made for each child with each of the child's nicknames their dad gave them on the back. I see them wearing them sometimes, and I am sure it's when they feel they need to have a part of their dad with them.

Running helps me to deal better and be calmer and not so afraid of life and what is to come. It's my rock, and it is part of me. I need it to live, to breathe. It's hard to explain to some people. It's not about exercise. It's just a part of me. I was born to run . . . so was Kevin.

Today, I don't feel the need to run away from my life anymore and constantly be on the go in hopes of escaping the pain. Now, because of my being at peace with what is, I don't feel the need to go, go, and go. I am okay with just being home. Initially, the children and I were always trying to escape this new life. We would often spend every weekend with my brother, Jeff, and his family. They were kind enough to allow us to be a part of their family. It made me feel more complete with mine. Also, we would go with my mom to California to be with my twin sister, Suzanne, and her family or to Florida to be with my younger sister, Jennifer, and her family quite a bit. Again, it was my/our way of surviving and escaping our new life. Plus, my older sister, Laura, and her family would meet us at some sort of play area, and Uncle Richard was always up for a trip and change of scenery. Just having someone else with us made me feel more normal and helped me to not focus on what was now missing—Kevin.

It took a lot of time and therapy to feel comfortable and safe at home again. For it was no longer our home together, it was no longer the home where we would raise our children and eventually grow old together. It didn't have the same meaning to me after Kevin died, but somehow, with all the help I sought, it does feel like home again for the children and me. Of course, there are still moments when I wish I had Kevin to share in the special moments and responsibilities of three children along with all the important decisions I have to make in life, but somehow, I have managed.

Initially, my enthusiasm and spirit for life died with Kevin, but now I actually enjoy life again. If there is one thing I could change, of course that would be to bring Kevin back. Sometimes I allow my mind to go there, to what might have been if Kevin had lived, but not very often because it is unhealthy. For that will never be. As Michele said, I gave him a great ending to his life, a legacy, and he gave me a great foundation for the rest of my life. Also, one of my therapists, Denise DeMarco, said to me, "Instead of you feeling like a part of you died with Kevin, you should feel a part of him lives on through the children and you." Kevin will always live on through his children. As for a part of me dying with Kevin, I know I am not exactly the same person I was before November 3, 2006. However, 90 percent of me is back. There will forever be a part of me that has changed. It's only normal to be a changed or different person once you go through the devastation of grief. The one part of me that stayed constant and still remains the same is the runner in me, that runner Kevin fell in love with. That will never be taken away.

Kevin lives on through each of our children in their own way. He truly is a part of who each of them is and have become. When I look at each of them, I can see their dad living on in them, most especially in our son, Quintin. He is so much his father. At one of Quintin's middle school basketball games, a coach from the opposing team came up to him and said, "I used to coach with your dad, and he was a great man. The intensity that you play with reminds me of him, and I love that you are so competitive, just like your dad. You are a good little player, Little Gatons." It is so nice that people still remember Kevin and that he truly lives on and will continue to live on for generations to come.

Over the last twelve years, the children and I have had our struggles, and I know we will continue to have them. There will always be moments of missing Kevin, but now, the moments don't consume us like they did in the beginning. We have all learned to accept our new life without Kevin. It is heartbreaking when the children have their struggles, and it is heartbreaking when I allow myself to imagine how different their little lives and mine would have been if Kevin didn't die.

I have learned over the years to not go there too often. It's not good for any of us. For the most part, life is good—just not what I envisioned it would be. Never did I imagine the person I would fall in love with would die so young or that our children would grow up without their dad. It's not the life I thought I would have if I made good choices, and not the life I thought I could plan. I am sure I am not alone in feeling this way and that many of you feel that your life didn't turn out as planned either.

I only got to be married for eight years; I wanted to be married to Kevin for the rest of my life. I know I am blessed to have had that for eight years, for some people never have it at all, but selfishly, that wasn't enough. I wanted it forever. As Alfred Lord Tennyson said, "'Tis better to have loved and lost than never to have loved at all." I had those words etched on the front of Kevin's headstone because I do feel blessed to have been loved by Kevin and to have loved him. Meeting Kevin changed my life forever and for the better. I would never change having met him, fallen in love with him, married him, and had children with him. I know that was all meant to be. I just wish our love story had a different ending, one where we grew old together.

On the back of the headstone, I had two runners etched in the stone to symbolize the two of us and the bond we shared. That love of running created our destinies.

I will continue to make good choices like I did with Kevin and see where the rest of my life leads me. I will also continue running this most important race, life. I know there will be moments when I feel like I am hitting the wall, just like in the marathon, but I will pick myself up and keep on running. I am not afraid to finish this race (to die), but I know I have a lot of running to do before I get to the finish because I have three children who need me. I know that when I cross the finish line, my two biggest fans, Kevin and my dad, will be there, cheering me on, smiling, and giving me the biggest hug. They will be most proud that I was able to finish this race. The hardest race I ever ran—my life.

In the meantime, I have a lot of living left to do, like Sia says in her song "Alive," "I survived, I'm still breathing, I'm still breathing, I'm still breathing, I'm still breathing, I'm alive, I'm alive, I'm *alive . . .* "

In one of my final visits to Michele, Kevin came through and said, "A toast to who we were, who you are, and who you will be." That made me smile and cry.

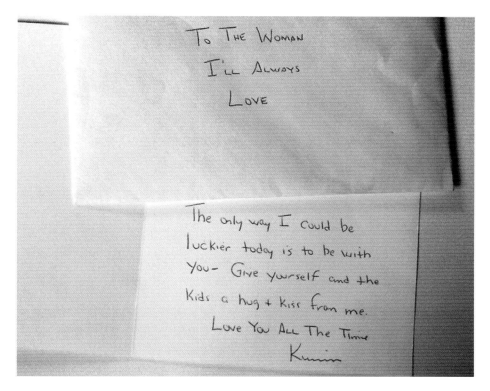

A cherished card Kevin left for me to find while he was running in Boston.

As for what the miles ahead entail, I am not exactly sure. I do, however, hope that despite the bends, curves, uphills, and downhills I encounter, I keep running and smiling along the way. For you never know what lies around the next bend. Maybe another chance at love or a new career once my children are grown or the opportunity to watch my children have the life I thought I would have. Just maybe that is why I always preferred a rolling course versus a flat course. I loved the variety, the excitement, and the challenges they offered. The uphills made me work harder, but the downhills allowed for recovery, while the curves and bends provided some twists and turns that enhanced the run. Just like in life.

Acknowledgments

To all of those whose lives have not turned out exactly how they thought, you too can go so much farther than 26.2 miles.

- Mom, Dad would be so proud of how far you have gone! I love you always, and I, too, am so proud of how far you have gone! Thank you for loving us.

- To all of those who were rooting and praying for the children and me, thank you is not enough!

- A special thanks to my friends: Annette Wu (the first friend I met through running and who also was a widow at a young age), Tammy Slusser, Lauren Henzler, and Chris Simpson (Chris, like Kevin, died way too young, tragically killed by a drunk driver. . . . I hope someday to run with her again in Heaven), who over many miles of running and conversations became dear friends who always rooted for me. Your friendships are another blessing that came to me through running. . . . Thank you.

- Special thanks to all who played a role in my survival, especially my therapists: Lynn Saxman, Monsignor Statnick, Denise DeMarco, Dr. Michele Reiss, and my emotional coach, Mie Elmhirst.

- Thanks to all the therapists that helped my children to get to a better place, especially Lori Iezzi.

- Thank you to the other young widows who reached out to me: Monica, Annette, Lisa, Carol, LuAnn, Gina, and Lynn. There are way too many of us.

- A special thanks to Coach Snider, Jeremy Lenzi, Frank Lehman, Barry Bupp, Tim Hewitt, Nathan Snider, and all those who volunteered, for their involvement in the Kevin Gatons' Memorial 5K. It was a wonderful way to honor Kevin and to allow those who knew Kevin to come together and heal through running.

- Stephanie and Todd Turin, thanks for always being there for me and my family. I will be forever grateful for your kindness and help and for treating us like family.

- Flo Barclay Myers, thank you for helping me during those darkest of days and allowing me moments of peace by watching the children so I could run. I appreciate all you did for us.

- Jim Schuck, thank you for sharing your story about being a young widower. Your letters of inspiration and kind words of encouragement gave me hope that someday I, too, would be in a better place and smile again.

- Thank you to all those who have remembered Kevin through races: Turkey Trot; Baldwin Invitational; The Red, White & Blue Race; etc. Thank you.

- Thank you on behalf of Kevin for recognizing his running accomplishments and inducting him into The St. Vincent's Hall of Fame and the Pittsburgh Marathon Hall of Fame.

- Thank you to Coach Dennis Clawson (Kevin's middle school basketball coach) for taking the time to meet with our children and for sharing with them stories about their dad as a young man.

- A special note of thanks to both my family and Kevin's: I appreciate all you do for us.

- Thank you to my sister Laura, husband, Joe, and family; my twin sister, Suzanne, husband, Jay, and family; my brother, Jeff, wife, Carla, and family; and my sister Jen, husband, Phillip, and family for allowing us to be a part of yours at times. In those moments, my family didn't feel so incomplete.

- Thank you to all my aunts, uncles, and grandparents for always rooting for me when I was competing and for now rooting for me in life. I greatly appreciate your support and love you!

- Thank you to Kevin's mom (Patricia) and dad (Terrence), sister Sue and husband, Barry, sister Beth and husband, Mark, and brother, Mike, and wife, Fe, for loving our children the way you do.

- John Gootz, you have been more than a handyman over the last twelve years. You always say, "If you need anything, call me." I do call, and you always come. Thanks for caring about the children and me. Your reliable friendship has been a gift, and Kevin would be so appreciative of all you have done for us. God definitely sent you to be in our lives. . . . Thanks so much.

- Michele Dugan, thank you for sharing your gift with me and allowing me closure. You will never know how much you helped me. I am forever grateful to you and your friendship. Please know that you truly are one of the reasons I survived it all.

- Thank you to the Moyer Foundation for creating Camp Erin (a youth bereavement camp), which allowed my children to gather with other children and share in their losses while having fun and creating special friendships. My children greatly benefited from their time there and realized that they weren't alone in experiencing the loss of a parent.

- Monica Green Fonseca, thank you for always being there for me and for understanding how I felt while you were experiencing your own loss. Your friendship has been a blessing. I only wish we had met under happier circumstances. Thank you for letting me realize through your newfound happiness that the glass can be half full again.

- Suzanne, my twin sister/best friend, I remember you saying to me that you feared you had lost your twin sister, but with your love and caring, along with the help of others, I was able to find my way back to 90 percent of the person I was prior to Kevin's and Dad's dying. Love you and thank you!

- A heartfelt thank you to my sorority sisters for always loving me.

- Richard Kurtz, Uncle Richard/Rick, thank you for putting your life on hold to help us survive ours. Words aren't enough . . . thank you. We are forever grateful for all you did to help us survive.

- Mark Schwartz, thanks for always caring and cheering me on.

- A final thanks to Coach Rich Wright for being there with Kevin when I couldn't and when he needed someone the most. . . . Thanks isn't even enough. . . . I feel blessed that Kevin had you with him in that final moment. He knew he wasn't alone. . . . Thank you.

- To Joe Sarver and Robert Sevene (Sev), thank you for being more than coaches. Thank you for being like family, for believing in me from day one, and thank you for helping me achieve all I did with my running. You two are the epitome of coaches who coach simply because they love the sport of running and because they want to help others reach their goals/dreams. I did just that because of the two of you.

- Joe Sarver, you have always been there for me through the happiest and saddest of times. You are one of the most important men in my life. By knowing you and your believing in me, my life took a different path. A path that led to so many amazing moments, most especially meeting Kevin. Thank you from the bottom of my heart for all the time you have dedicated to me over the years. I treasure our coach/athlete relationship but even more so the family you have become to me.

- Judy Sarver, Danielle Sarver Pinkerton, and Janine Sarver Dyson, thank you for treating me like family and for sacrificing time with your husband/dad so he could train me. I will be forever grateful.

- Sev, you have touched so many lives with your coaching, and I am just one of many who have been lucky enough to meet you, have been coached by you, and share a special friendship with you. I feel blessed that you are in my life.

- A special thanks to: Dr. Jane Crosson of Johns Hopkins, Crystal Tichnell, Johns Hopkins, and Children's Hospital of Pittsburgh for all you do for ARVD research and for our children being in good hands every three years when they get tested.

- Dr. Wayne Ross, pathologist of Harrisburg, Pennsylvania, thanks again for giving me answers when I so desperately needed them.

- Thanks to Debbie and Terry Bower for being there for us even through your own pain and for always caring about Kevin, the children, and me.

- Samantha Bower, thank you for helping me through the most difficult time of my life by sharing your pain and loss with me. You were a young athlete who Kevin loved coaching, and now you are a wonderful young lady who treasures life in ways others might not because of what happened November 3, 2006. Kevin would be so proud of the person you are and of your running achievements.

- To my dad, I love you and miss you. Thanks for being the best dad any little girl or adult women could have. I was *loved*. Your influence made me who I am. . . .

- To our children, you are the reason I survived the unthinkable. As sung in the song "He Lives in You" from *The Lion King*, "He [your dad] lives in you, he lives in me, he watches over everything we see, into the water, into the truth, in your reflection he lives in you." Sydney, Quintin, and Lillian, thank you for letting me continue to see glimpses of your dad and to know he is still here with us and always will be.

- To Kevin, thank you for choosing to love me and to share your life with me. I will love you for always and then some. . . .

One final note to our children:
May you have a fairy tale ending.

A Special Acknowledgement:

Before my book was able to go to print, my very good friend, Kathy Green Soisson, passed away at the young age of fifty-two. I had known Kathy since I was eighteen years old. We were lifelong friends. She came to my side the moment Kevin died and never left. Her strength as I state previously helped me through the most difficult time of my life. Twelve years later and now Kathy is no longer here. Life is extremely hard to understand at times. I am struggling with this loss but as I mentioned earlier it is God's plan and not ours. Kathy was very strong in her faith and would accept that God knew what was best for her and her family. I will always be thankful for her gift of friendship and will always miss and love her. She played a huge role in helping me to go "Farther Than 26.2 Miles".

Please, if you know of anyone who might show signs of ARVD, contact:

Crystal Tichnell, MGC
Genetic Counselor
ARVD Program
Johns Hopkins Hospital
600 N. Wolfe Street/Carnegie 530
Baltimore, MD 21287
P) 410-502-7161
F) 410-502-9148

My story was worth telling even if one life can be saved and others can be educated on ARVD to prevent someone, just like Kevin, from dying and spare all those who love that someone the heartache and pain I and all who loved Kevin experienced.

On our honeymoon in Aruba, August 1998. One of my favorite photos of Kevin.

August 2006 - Kevin's last birthday. He turned forty-six.

Sydney (five months) with Mom and Dad at her first track meet - April 2001.

Kevin holding Sydney (three and a half years old) after he
ran the Freedom 5K race. Fourth of July 2004.

Sydney, almost nine years old. Kevin Gatons's memorial kid race – 2009.

Kevin and Quintin (three months) - June 2003.

Kevin and baby Quintin – 2004.

Quintin, six years old. Kevin Gatons's memorial kid race – 2009.

Uncle Bob. Kevin. and Lilly – February 2006. Lilly's first birthday.

Kevin with Lilly (twenty months) - October 2006.

Lilly, four years old. Kevin Gatons's memorial kid race – 2009.

Kevin's parents, Terrence and Patricia Gatons, with Kevin
and me at Sydney's baptism (their first grandchild).

Sydney, Quintin, and Lillian with their cousins the summer after Kevin
died at Lake Edinboro. (Kids really do live in the moment) - June 2007.

Not so long ago, Lilly and I were sitting at a red light as a funeral procession went by. She asked me if we did that for her dad, and I said yes. I told her that I hated it and I was glad she didn't remember. She responded that she wished she remembered, and I asked her, "What?" She said her dad. My heart broke. . . .

A note Lilly gave me when she was six years old.

Eleven years after Kevin died, our son, Quintin, who was a soccer player, decided to quit the soccer team and run cross country. After his second meet, Michele (who had no idea about him quitting soccer) called me out of the blue with a message. She said, "Tell Quintin his dad is very proud of him. He should be pleased with the win, and come November, he needs to go and finish what his dad couldn't." Later that year, in November, eleven years to the date, Quintin ran in the Pennsylvania State Cross Country meet and finished what his dad couldn't at Hershey. (In that moment, his dad handed the torch off to Quintin as well.) His joining cross country has been a positive, and I feel things have come full circle. Hershey is now a happy place.

Twelve years to the date, the Greensburg Salem Boys' C.C. team won states. I am sure Kevin was smiling!

Quintin qualifying for the 2017 PA State Cross Country meet.

Sydney's First Prom – 2017.

There will always be moments of sadness (wishing their dad were here with us) mixed with moments of happiness. However, I, along with the children, will not allow the sadness to overtake the happiness, for I/we have gone *Farther Than 26.2 Miles.*

Without their assistance, this book would not be in your hands. A big "thank you" to them both!

Copy Editor: Corey Niles
Book/Cover Design: Darlene Patrick

Corey Niles is the literary poetry editor for *Eye Contact Magazine*. His most recent publications include "Buried" in *Under the Bed* magazine, "Beached" in *Deadman's Tome*, and "The Trailer" and "The Verge" in *Corvus Review*. He lives in Pennsylvania.

Darlene Patrick is a freelance graphic artist and paraeducator at a career and tech center for high school students. She is a partner with Caring Media International™, the creative founder of the award-winning program The Caring Habit Adventure™ and The 12 Habits for Wonderful People™, and illustrator of the book *Join the Golden Rule Revolution™*. She resides in Greensburg, Pennsylvania, with her husband, Jefferey, and considers her children, Heather, Ryan, and Samantha, her greatest work of art.

A special note of thanks to Kathrine Switzer for being the wonderful woman, role model, and person you are. Your kindness and time in helping me with my book is greatly appreciated. Your friendship is a gift. I am blessed to have met you and befriended you through my running. You were the first woman to officially run 26.2 miles, and because of you, the world of women's running has gone so much further than the 26.2 miles you ran that very day!

To all those I have met along the way and have touched my life through running; most especially Kevin,
THANK YOU.